MISSIE

MISSIE

THE LIFE AND TIMES OF
ANNIE OAKLEY

ANNIE FERN SWARTWOUT

COACHWHIP PUBLICATIONS

Greenville, Ohio

Missie: The Life and Times of Annie Oakley, by Annie Fern
    Swartwout
© 2013 Coachwhip Publications
No claims made on public domain material.
Published 1947. Additional photographs included in this
    edition.

ISBN 1-61646-217-5
ISBN-13 978-1-61646-217-8

CoachwhipBooks.com

CONTENTS

FOREWORD

FOR MORE THAN thirty years I spent a great deal of time with my mother's sister, the late Annie Oakley. Living and traveling with her I learned all of the interesting stories of her life.

When but a child I was thrilled with the story of how she learned to shoot in order to provide food for her family, and many times when I was supposed to be asleep I sat in the attic with an oil lamp by my side writing imaginary stories of her life, and later hid them under the boards of the attic floor.

I not only admired my aunt as a rare genius who had generated a new atmosphere that seemed impossible. The fact that she had risen from obscurity to eminence and had mastered serious difficulties in her upward climb made me love her peculiar qualities, and how this was done is shown in the pages of this book.

In the preparation of this volume the author has endeavored to present in a concrete and authentic form an accurate biography of her famous aunt, whom the people of all the world admired and loved for her simplicity of character so impervious to flattery, and so modest in her bearing. A woman of tireless energy, the most unselfish character I have ever known.

1
THE BIRTH OF ANNIE OAKLEY

IN A PIONEER log cabin in Darke County, Ohio, on the 13th day of August, 1860, a baby girl was born, the sixth to appear in the family of Susan and Jacob Moses, and the fifth living child. They called her Phoebe Ann, but the four older sisters, Mary Jane, Lydia, Elizabeth and Sarah Ellen, did not like this name and called her Annie, the name that clung to her the rest of her life. The cabin into which she had come was without luxuries and claimed very few comforts; but for all that, the first stages of the move into this new section had been accomplished before her arrival, and already much had been done to make the rough cabin habitable.

Built in haste five years before, the new home had at first only one room with a floor of hammered clay, but additional rooms were built on later as the size of the family demanded. Heat and cooking facilities came from one huge fireplace into which logs several feet long could be rolled so as to keep fire all night in cold weather. Wood was plentiful and could be had for the cutting, and furniture had been made by the resourceful head of the house. Altogether it was, according to pioneer standards, a comfortable, if not a pretentious home.

The little cabin stood on a farm about two miles north of Versailles, Ohio at a place then called Willow Dell and later Woodland. Cincinnati, about eighty miles away, was the nearest town of any size. This part of Ohio was chosen as a home by the Moses family, and many others, partly, at least, because it was low ground, and they had expected the water supply to be ample and easy to reach. It developed, on the contrary, that the water channels lay deep, and shallow wells, the only kind possible to pioneer skill and tools, ran dry in summer unless supplemented by rain-water caught in home-made barrels. Drainage, too, was difficult, and roads hard to build; but the farms, once drained, were productive, and swampy roads had to be endured.

It was not an easy life to which the new baby had come, and no one expected it to be, least of all in time to come the indomitable soul that lay now in its cradle. It was such stock, brave and un-daunted, that built an empire from sea to sea, and although the atom of humanity that had just arrived, and that was to be Annie Oakley some day, lived to enjoy the luxury of Courts, she never ceased to be the sturdy child of the new world, living out her life under canvas and in the open.

Annie's clever mind and strong personality were manifested very early. Her beauty, too, was striking and of a type suggestive of race. Somewhere in the family line, parents or grandparents, or farther back, lies the reason for this heritage; but of her forbears not a great deal is known. Enough to be suggestive, however.

Her parents, Susan and Jacob Moses, had come into Ohio from Pennsylvania where they had been keeping an Inn on the route followed by the covered wagons going West. This prospered until a fire destroyed both Inn and savings, and then they had made this new start in Ohio, led on to the venture, no doubt, by the travelers who stopped at the door of their Inn. The journey was a matter of swamps and corduroy roads, and they took their three children with them. The usual frontier virtues are here, but the records tell us little more. Of Jacob Moses we know little, although the name was a good one in our early history; of Susan, a little more. She seems to have been an unhappy and ill-treated little drudge, a sort of American Cinderella when Jacob Moses lifted her to his saddle and rode away with her at fifteen and married her. She was the daughter of Emily and Jacob Wise, who also kept an Inn near Hollidaysburg, Pennsylvania. Again Wise is a good name in our history, and one wonders about a certain early Governor of Virginia, but again there is no proof. Emily was the daughter of Jacob and Ellenor Clapper, who came to America in 1764; but back of that we know little of the family. There are implications aplenty, but there seems to be no record.

When Annie was two years old there was again a new baby in the crowded little cabin—a boy this time at last, and the family's cup of joy had been filled. They named him John. Once more, when Annie was four and hoping, above all things, for another girl baby, sure enough the old stork brought one; and Annie thought her then, and always afterward, the best of all sisters. They called her Hulda, and with this child the family was complete. Hulda Moses was my mother.

Seven children made it necessary to increase the size of the cabin. Beds were made and fitted with homespun ticks filled with straw. Susan Moses never wasted a scrap of anything, and all the patches of cloth she could save were made into comforters to be used on the beds as they needed them. Everything in the log cabin was as clean as could be, and everything was kept in its place, so at all times the house looked its best.

Although the father worked early and late, the family fortunes did not seem to increase until he secured a Government position carrying the mail from Greenville to the small towns as far north as Woodland. This meant traveling a long distance on horseback through the swampy country in all kinds of weather, but it meant too, a small regular income to help care for this family of growing children. Meanwhile, of course, there was much to be done at home with the help of his wife and children. Grain and vegetables must be raised on the farm; game was abundant, but must be shot or trapped. The cow that grazed in the woods through the summer months, and that furnished them with milk and butter, had to be cared for and milked.

Nuts were plentiful—hickory, hazel, butter and black walnuts. Wild strawberries, raspberries and blackberries were a welcome change in diet, even though eaten without sugar, for sugar was scarce and expensive. Nuts and berries could be had for the gathering, and this was a task for farm children. As snakes lay sunning themselves lazily among the bushes, Annie's mother warned the small nut and berry pickers not to go too far from the farm.

The wilderness lay just beyond the Moses' inclosure, a prolific wilderness, but a menacing one too. In the winter hungry wolves came out of the forest, and it was always necessary to keep the children near the cabin. Even wild cats were present, and on one occasion one tried to jump to the horse's back as the father was returning to his home from delivering the mail. The horse sensed the danger and gave a quick jump to one side, just in time to let the cat fall to the ground, and by the time he had recovered sufficiently to pursue, the horse was well on his way to a farmhouse that was near. When the cat saw the light from the house, he turned and lost himself in the forest.

Indians were no longer a danger by the time Annie was born, although Indian warfare had lasted over a longer period in that section of Ohio than in any other part of the country. In fact, the famous Treaty of Greenville that finally brought a lasting peace, was signed in 1795 not twenty miles from the Moses farm. Many Indian stories were, of course, current at that time and place, and Annie's interest in Indians began very early.

Thus the forest lay around the farm, but culture and education from the outside world were creeping toward them from the East. The churches and schools were far apart, and hard to reach. Susan Moses was a Quakeress, and as there was no Quaker Meeting Place in this part of the country, the family rarely attended church in Annie's childhood. The nearest school was two miles away, too far for small children; so consequently Annie's early education was sadly neglected, although efforts in that direction were made by herself and by her family and friends, as will appear later. Even the neighborhood cabins were scattered, but, pioneer fashion, the families clung together, and a neighbor could be depended upon to help in emergencies for there was no one else to help. In those black years that began when Annie was five and lasted until she was ten, the kindness of this or that neighbor was all that made life endurable for them all.

Thus the outside world touched them but little. These were the war years, 1860 to 1865. Lincoln was elected President, and the war between the States wore on through four bitter years. Lincoln was assassinated, and the Nation mourned. Reconstruction began in the South that seemed almost worse than the war. Far away in Europe Queen Victoria reigned in England, Alexander II in Russia, and William I in Germany. All this would mean much to Annie some day, but not now. In this isolated little cabin even the Civil War seemed to have come and gone, without leaving its mark,— Jacob Moses was over the age for service; and the struggle for existence continued to occupy all of their time.

It was in the Fall of 1865 when the bitterest years of Annie's life began with a disaster which was crushing to the whole family. It happened in this way: The mill where they had grain ground, was a long way from Woodland and it took all day to make the journey both ways with a wagon and team of horses, so the trip was not made very often. In the late Fall when Annie was five, her father started one morning with wheat and corn to be ground for the winter supply. The sky looked dark and threatening, but he kissed the family and was off, for he thought that winter would possibly set in at any time, and he might as well brave the storm one time as another. It was always a long, hard trip over the rough roads when they were at their best, but during that day a terrific blizzard set in, and it took him longer than usual to reach the mill. He left the wheat and corn to be ground, and went to the General Store to buy the supply of groceries for the winter, as well as the few other things in the way of clothing he could afford. He then returned for the flour and meal with the bran to be used for mash for the cow.

The storm raged, the wind howled and the snow fell thick and fast, but he started back. He could not think of being away over night, even if it should be very late before he reached his home and loved ones. The faithful horses plodded on and on, as the snow grew deeper and deeper. He knew that at home the big logs in the fireplace would still be burning, and that a warm welcome awaited him. It was after midnight when the horses drew up near enough to the house that Susan waiting anxiously could hear the noise of the wagon through the howling wind. She threw open the door, in the face of the blizzard, and as the light streamed out she saw her good husband sitting stiffly on the box, the reins thrown around his neck for his hands were too numb to hold them any longer. "Thank God he's here," she said, and plunged out into the storm to help him in. His speech was almost gone, and he was not far from death, but the horses had somehow found their way alone through the blinding, blinding storm.

His wife and oldest daughter carried him into the house and laid him on the bed they had made in front of the fireplace, for they had known that he would be very cold when he reached home. The mother brought whiskey in a cup of hot water, and gave him a spoonful at a time until he began to revive and feel a little warmth in his almost frozen body. Meanwhile the daughters rubbed his hands and feet with snow to bring back the blood that was so chilled. All night long his mind wandered while the mother and oldest daughter, Mary Jane, watched by his bedside.

The other girls managed to get the horses into the shed, and blanketed and fed them. They carried the flour and corn meal with the bran, and all of the other things for winter use into the house and stored them in the attic. Jacob Moses had paid dearly for these things; the family breadwinner had provided for his family for the last time—he never made another trip with the mail, and the small income from the Government was no longer a help. It proved to be a long, hard winter, and the family entered upon a period of stress that lasted many months.

During the long winter days the father grew steadily worse until in March, 1866, after the first few warm days came, the weather changed to a damp, cold wind, and he developed pneumonia and in three days the pain was more than he could stand, and God opened the gates to Paradise and his spirit entered the other world. Thus the little widow was left with the task of providing for a family of seven children, the eldest but fifteen years old.

2
ANNIE'S BROTHER LEFT WITH RESPONSIBILITY

THE MOTHER was a good nurse, but all she could earn was one dollar and a quarter a week taking care of maternity cases, and she usually had to do all of the housework and cooking for the family. In order to be able to work, Susan had to find someone who was willing to take care of the youngest child, baby Hulda. So she let a family by the name of Bartholmew take the dearest of all her children. For six years they cared for her as their very own child. The separation was almost more than Annie could stand, for she had loved her baby sister more than anyone else in the world, and had taken a great deal of care of her. When she was taken away, Annie was so lonely for her she became ill. A dear friend promised to take care of John when the mother and Mary Jane could get anything to do, and in that way they could both work. Annie was then nearly seven, and a very independent child who could do a lot of things for herself.

Mary Jane was a good girl and was glad to be able to take care of the younger children. Sometimes she too could earn a little as a practical nurse for maternity cases. As the eldest girl, she was for a short time a great help to her mother; but another tragedy was in store for them. Less than a year from the time of her father's death she was employed upon a case, when as night drew on the father of the infant so terrified the young girl that she left his house without adequate clothing against the weather which was cold and wet, and walked three miles through the woods to her home. In

15

places she waded water to her knees, and arrived with her clothing drenched through. She was taken with tuberculosis and died in five months, a little more than a year after her father's death, leaving her mother with a little more sorrow and care.

With these added burdens Susan could not pay the lease on the farm, and had to give up the place she had hoped to someday own. Almost everything was sold to pay doctor bills and funeral expenses. Even "Old Pink," the cow, had to be sold, for it took the money she would bring to finish paying the bills. A kind neighbor had built a new house for himself, and he offered Susan and her family his old log house to live in. They were glad for the kind offer, and made the old log cabin as comfortable as they could with what they had left.

That year was a hard one for them all. It was that fall that Annie learned to fill her small stomach by the use of her clever head. Quail were plentiful, and Annie learned to trap them. She made traps of heavy cornstalks laid up like log houses and tied together with heavy string; she dug a small trench and set the trap over it at one end, then covered the trap with brush sufficient to hide it. She fixed it up like a brush-heap, which was protection from wild animals that might eat the birds after caught. For there were plenty of muskrat, raccoon, and even opossum, that would be glad to feast upon the birds without having to catch them for themselves.

Annie scattered corn along the bottom of the trench into the traps, thus the little brown birds were tempted into the traps. She kept several traps set, and in this way provided some meat for the family. The birds were served in different ways, broiled, roasted, and sometimes fricasseed with potpie. While Annie was trying to trap the quail, she was always wondering how long it would be before she could use the forty-inch cap and ball Kentucky rifle that had been her father's.

During the winter a stray cow came to them. No one seemed to know to whom the cow belonged, and she seemed to be glad enough to get into a warm shed during the cold winter and have some feed while the snow covered the ground. But when spring came and she had a calf, she was cross and would not let anyone milk her if she could help it. But the Moses family thought it worthwhile if they could get her into the corral to get a little milk now and then.

One day the mother was away at work and Annie could not wait another day to shoot the gun she had so longed to try. She climbed upon the bench by the side of the fireplace so that she could reach the gun that hung over the mantelpiece. She took down the gun, powder-horn and the bag of shot. When she loaded the muzzle-loader she made the mistake of doing it in front of the fireplace. When her mother came home and started to build a fire she swept the ashes that were on the hearth back into the fireplace, and the powder sparked in the hot ashes. At once Susan knew someone had been trying to load the gun. When she asked whom it might be Annie admitted it and told her mother that if she would only let her, she knew she could shoot rabbits they could eat.

That was the beginning of Annie's shooting career that astounded not only her friends, but the whole world and was the means of her becoming the most famous woman of her time. Later she was able to hold audiences of thousands of people spellbound by her unusual skill.

Annie was able to shoot enough game to provide fresh meat for the family at a time when otherwise it would have been impossible for them to have bought the food they needed so badly.

As spring came on, provisions grew lower and lower; at times they made gravy out of flour and water, with a little salt, and ate it on homemade bread, and thought they had a meal.

One morning just before daybreak, Annie heard talking outside. She got up and looked out of the window to see if she could find out whom it might be. It was her mother kneeling on the ground outside with her face turned toward the rising sun; her eyes were closed and her hands were clasped as she prayed these words, "Oh God, I know Thou art with us; I need bread and meat to feed my children. Thou wilt not desert us. Amen." The children had eaten the last bread and meat the night before, and all there was in the house to eat was a cup of flour and a handful of salt.

Not long after daybreak someone thought they heard a wagon coming down the road that had not thawed out, for it was spring and the mud-roads would freeze at night and stay frozen until the sun came up to thaw the mud. As the old spring-wagon came near, all eyes were watching to see where it might be going so early in the morning, when to their great surprise the driver turned the horse into the lane that led to their house. Annie was the first one to open the door and rush out to welcome the old neighbor who called out to her mother, "Good morning Susie. Thought I'd come over to see how you was. I've some flour I won't need 'til time to harvest the wheat, and more meat than I'll use 'til time to butcher in the fall. You know two more of my children got married last winter, and we ain't eat so much as usual." The old fellow pulled a ham and some bacon out from under the seat of the old spring wagon, and unloaded a few bags of flour, and told her that his brother would bring over some potatoes he was not going to use, and said, "Guess you can use them, can't you?"

The children were all delighted with the flour and meat, for they knew their mother was worried about what they were going to eat that day. They were all standing around to hear what the neighbor had to say when Annie suddenly thought she would try to milk the wild cow, and in that way have some milk for breakfast. About the time the neighbor was ready to leave they heard Annie scream, and they all rushed to the back of the house in time to see her dodge behind the frame of a big grindstone to get out of the way of the wild cow. Old Black thought she would put an end to the milking business once and for always, so she was trying to kill Annie. The child, of course, was rescued from the horns of the angry animal.

Dan Brumbaugh was shocked to see that Susan and the girls were having such a hard time. All the way home he wondered what he could do about it. In a few days he had it all settled in his own mind. He had been thinking about all of his own children being married—his wife had been dead for several years—and he thought of the lonely years ahead of him. So one day he got all dressed up in his best, and drove over to see what Susie, as he called her, thought about sharing his cows, for he had plenty of everything. He told her it was dangerous to have those girls milking that stray cow, and that there was no need of it if she were willing to share his everything.

Susan thought it not such a bad idea, and they were soon married. Things now looked as if they were going to straighten out, and that life might be a little easier for the whole family. Everyone worked hard and planned for a happy future.

The children were in school, but the family that had taken Hulda had become so attached to her they begged to keep her, with the promise she could visit her own family often. For at that time, Bartholmew's were a prosperous family, so Hulda had escaped in this way the hardship and poverty endured by Annie and the rest of her family.

Dan had rented his farm to one of his sons, and as soon as the son could find a place to buy, Dan intended to move the family over to the big farm where they would have a modern, comfortable place. Just before it was time to move, disaster struck again. Dan was taken ill and died, leaving Susan with another baby girl five months old. Emily, was her name. Again the older girls loved her and tried to do their best for her, for she was their baby sister. With very few toys to play with, a baby to take care of was always welcome, and to take the place of the beautiful dolls girls now have.

After the death of Susan's second husband, some of his children that were married helped her some with the burden of her family, which was at that time not light, and the families have remained friends for generations down to the present time.

3
ANNIE STARTS TO EARN HER WAY

SUSAN HAD TO MAKE some new plans, and her family was again separated. She let Annie, then about eight years old, go to stay with a friend, a Mrs. Eddington, for part of the summer. But one of the Eddington children came down with scarlet fever, and Annie took the dreaded disease and very nearly died. Upon her recovery, Mrs. Eddington, greatly concerned, for she felt in a measure it had been her fault that Annie had so nearly lost her life, decided Annie had better stay with her all winter, for if she were to go home she would have nearly two miles to walk to school. She could go to school with the Eddington children and come home to lunch, and after having been so ill Mrs. Eddington felt it was important for such a frail little girl to have every chance to grow strong again. With Susan away at work part of the time, it would be hard for Annie to have the proper care and have such a long way to walk through the deep snow.

Annie proved to be a great help to Mrs. Eddington, for her husband was Superintendent of the County Infirmary where both old people and children were cared for at that time. Annie loved the Eddington baby, and took care of him as much as she could. Mrs. Eddington grew very fond of Annie, and did everything she could to make her happy. She taught her to sew, and before spring came Annie had learned to make dresses for the children that were in the Home. She was allowed to sew on the new sewing machine, and that was a great inspiration to her, for the sewing she had learned to do at home was all done by hand—Annie's mother had never been able to afford a sewing machine.

21

More than once Annie finished a garment late on a Saturday night so some small child could wear it to Sunday School on Sunday.

Mrs. Eddington was so fond of Annie she thought it would be even better for her to be in a private home than to be associated with the children in the County Home, so she wrote to Annie's mother telling her what a great help Annie had been to her, and how she had learned to sew and care for the small children, and asked what she should do about keeping her after school was out in the Spring.

Before Mrs. Eddington had a chance to hear from Annie's mother, a farmer came to the Home and asked if he could get a girl that could help care for a small baby. Annie was present and heard the conversation. She thought at once of the money she might be able to earn, and asked if she might not try to take care of the child. Mrs. Eddington knew Annie was capable, and said she might try working for the farmer's wife for two weeks, and if she liked it and they liked her, she might stay all summer if her mother thought the plan all right, and that she would write to her mother and let her know. Susan's reply was that if Annie was happy and really wanted to work, and if Mrs. Eddington thought the farmer's wife would be good to Annie, she might try it until school started in the fall.

Unfortunately, none of these well-meaning people looked into the home to which the poor child was now going. If they had, the bitterest two years of Annie's five years of tragedy might have been spared her, and an experience that altered her character for life.

Annie never called the family that she went to by its name. She always referred to them as the "wolves," and said they were wolves in sheep's clothing. To distinguish these people from families whose name was really "Wolf," Annie in later years spelled the name without a capital letter, and in her unfinished autobiography she so writes them down. So it was that Annie went into the world to earn a living at nine, and a hard world she found it, poor child.

After Annie reached the Wolf farm they found out she was willing, and so anxious to help her mother that she would work from early until late as hard as she could, and would do anything they asked her to do. The Wolf family made it rather pleasant for her the first two weeks, until after they had written to the Eddingtons of how satisfied Annie was, and that they wanted to keep her all summer. Then the whole family helped to pile up work every day. She got up at four o'clock in the morning in order to have breakfast for the family. She had sliced ham or bacon, pared and fried potatoes, and sometimes fried corn meal mush that she had made the night before. Sometimes she baked biscuits and had made coffee and set the table by the time the family were ready for breakfast. After breakfast was over she rushed to the barn to milk at least two cows, she carried the milk to the house and strained it, and put it in the spring-house. She skimmed the yesterday's milk and fed it to the calves, and carried milk and water to the pigs. She washed the dishes and rocked the baby to sleep; and by that time it was time to get dinner. And that was no small task, for in the summer she gathered vegetables from the garden and prepared them. By that time Mrs. Wolf got around to help a little. After dinner Annie washed the dishes, and then it was time to rock the baby some more.

Day after day she toiled from early until late, and thought she was doing the thing she should do—and this all for fifty cents a week, which she believed the farmer was sending to her mother. When fall came and it was time for Annie to go to school, the wolves wrote to her mother telling her how happy Annie was and that she wanted to stay and go to school from their house, and that they would give her the clothes she needed and buy her books. Annie's mother, relieved that her child was so advantageously provided for, wrote that there was no reason why she should not stay. If only the too-trusting Susan had known the facts! The facts were that the schoolhouse was two miles from the farm, and with all of the work Annie was supposed to do before she went to school, she rarely went at all. The only chance she had to study was to prop a book upon the table while she washed the dishes, and then if the Mrs. wolf caught her, she would have to put the book away.

One winter night after the work was done, Annie was given a pile of stockings to mend. She worked until after nine o'clock and her eyes would not stay open another minute. Tired from her day's toil she fell asleep. When the Mrs. wolf looked around and found she was not at work, she struck the child so hard that she cried with pain, then she caught her by the arm and threw her out into the cold kitchen, and when she could not stop crying the old wolf thrust her out of the kitchen door. About the time Annie was so cold she hardly knew what to do, she heard footsteps; it was the wolf himself coming from some debate that had been held in the schoolhouse. Mrs. wolf tried to explain what had happened, and ordered her up-stairs where she slept in an old trundle-bed in one corner of a large room that was as cold as the kitchen had been.

All night long Annie was delirious at times and cried out in her sleep, and when she did some member of the heartless family would come to her and shake her back to reason. In her conscious moments she sobbed and wondered how much longer she could endure the heavy work and the blows that were worse than the work. She tried to plan how she could get away from the hard-hearted people who were holding her, almost as a prisoner.

The next morning she was allowed to rest for a little while with no food, until she could venture to crawl down the cold stairs. With her sister, Hulda, and her mother uppermost in her mind, she asked Mrs. wolf to take her home. The answer was with a chuckle, "No! If you ask again, I will cut your liver and heart out and hang them on the fence for the crows to eat."

Annie was almost forty miles from home, and that was a long distance when she did not have a penny; and her mother thought she was so happy she did not want to go home. All the time the wolves had been writing her mother telling her that Annie was going to school, and that she was so happy that she did not talk of going home. At the same time they read letters to her that her mother was supposed to have written to Annie telling her to stay and be a good little girl for she needed the money so badly. Little did Annie think that the wolves had written these letters themselves.

The few neighbors were sorry for Annie and were concerned, wondering what they could do to get her away from the people that were making her do work that was too hard for a child so young.

But they were afraid to do anything about it, for they knew they would be in trouble with the cruel people if they tried to interfere, and there was no law at that time to protect children.

Annie wearied through the remainder of the winter without going to school more than a week or two, and when spring came there was more work than ever for her frail little hands to do. The wolves had planned a trip for themselves, to be gone two weeks. Instructions were given Annie how to keep the gates closed, how to take care of the stock, and just what to do with the butter she churned, as well as how to do all of the spring house-cleaning. For a girl of ten it was more than she could do, try as hard as she would. As usual, she worked hard and did everything as best she could, for she had been promised a visit with her mother as soon as the farmers returned.

When the wolves returned they brought a bride and groom with them. The bride was a sister of Mr. wolf. That meant a little more hard work for Annie. Mrs. wolf seemed satisfied with all of the work Annie had done, so again she ventured to ask if she might not go home for the visit that had been promised to her when the wolves returned. She promised that she would be back in a week or two. Mrs. wolf gave her a grin and with a twist of her lips she hissed, "Don't you dare ask to go home." When Annie reminded her of her promise, the grin returned and she said, "I just wanted to make sure everything would be taken care of while we were away." Needless to say, that night Annie sobbed herself to sleep. She stood it two more days, and she was ill when the wolves left for the day to take the bride and groom to visit with some relatives. There was the usual day's work to be done, and a big basket of clothes was left for her to iron. The child ironed for two hours, and then the daring thought came to her, "Why not run away?"

Hurriedly she put her scant supply of ragged clothes in a pile and tied them up, and started to walk to the nearby town where she could get a train that would take her within a few miles from where her mother had lived when she left home to go to the Eddingtons. As she hurried along she passed a house not far from the railroad station, and a voice called to her, "Stop Annie, where are you going?" It was a little girl she knew. Annie stopped long enough to tell her friend that she was running away, that she no longer could stay away from her mother and endure the life at the wolf farm. Annie's friend took her into her home and told the story to her mother. The woman asked if she had enough money to pay her fare home on the train. Annie told her she had intended to ask the conductor if he would let her ride free; that she would pay him sometime. The kind woman gave the poor frightened little girl money for her train fare, and with it she gave her a lunch to eat on the train, for she knew Annie would not get home until after dark and that she could not help being hungry before then. The little friend and her mother walked to the train with Annie, and assured her that they were glad she was going to get away at last from the family that had almost killed her because they had made her so unhappy and had made her work so hard.

In those days people often took children into their homes to make drudges out of them, for they knew there was no one to look after the treatment of such children, and the laws were not yet in effect that could protect them. They told such children they should be glad to work for their board and clothing. Often they provided but scant supply of clothing.

Once Annie was on the train she shared a seat with a kindly old gentleman who asked her where she was going, and the usual question asked of children—how old she was. The lonely, frightened little girl seemed to have confidence in him at once. She told him she was ten years old, and that she was running away from where she had been working nearly two years. She told him, too, that she was so glad to be going home to her mother and sisters and brother, but wondered if she might be doing wrong to run away. The old gentleman reassured her on this point. One can fancy what strong opinions and sulphurous thoughts he must have had regarding the wolves, if Annie told him but half the truth. When the conductor came for the tickets, Annie's new friend told him that he would pay her fare, but the conductor (he must have overheard at least part of the conversation) smiled and said, "No fare for the child. I hope she reaches her mother safely." Annie settled back in relief and continued her journey and her conversation with the old gentleman. Recollecting some stick-candy he happened to have in his traveling case, he opened it and gave Annie some. She thanked him, but told him she would keep it for her little brother and sisters at home. This from a child of ten who had probably not tasted such a delicacy in the last two years or longer! We wonder if the old gentleman did not perhaps have trouble with his throat and blew his nose vigorously when this happened. Two strangers who within the short space of her journey fell victim to the charm of a shabby, neglected little waif. It was a greater tribute to Annie Oakley's character than the effortless ease with which she later captivated Princes and potentates when she was a beautiful and glamorously successful woman in her twenties.

The years of tragedy were over, although the child could not know that yet, but with a child's hopefulness, she sensed it, and as she left the train and her kind friend she was so happy with the thought that she would soon be with her loved ones again that her heart leaped for joy. The sun was a little brighter than usual, and the grass seemed to be more brilliant green, for it was still spring and everything in the country was beautiful.

Not until later did she realize that the kind gentleman who had slipped away on the train, had gone out of her life forever. She had neglected to ask him his name, and in later years she wondered many times who he might have been, and wished he could know how much he had encouraged her the day she was going home to her mother. She would have liked him to know of her success in life, and to have been able to return a good deed would have given her a great deal of pleasure. But then, she could think only of what was before her.

The train left the station and Annie was alone on the station platform. She looked about to get her bearings, for some improvements had been made. A new shed and platform had been built to the station that made her wonder if she had gotten off at the right place. She soon located some other buildings which gave her assurance she was all right, and then she started to walk in the direction of her home. She had about four miles to walk. She carried her little bundle first in one arm, then in the other, and the bag with the stick-candy under the string—for if she carried it in her hand, she was afraid she might eat it, or it might melt, and she did so want to have the candy when she got home. She knew the only time the children ever had candy was at Christmas.

As Annie hurried along her way she wondered what changes she would find when she got home, and with the elasticity of childhood the experiences she had on the wolf farm had already begun to seem like a bad dream she might have had. She soon came to a house where she knew the people, and thought she would stop in and inquire about her family, and get a drink. She knew she could not stay long because she would have to hurry along if she were to get home before dark.

The old neighbor told Annie of the marriage of her mother to a Mr. Shaw, and said his daughter was a "War Widder," and that she had three children, and that they got pensions from the Government. Annie knew Mr. Shaw, and knew the family would be well cared for if he had anything to do with providing for them. She was more anxious than ever to get home and see what changes had taken place, but she was several miles from the new home, so the old neighbor insisted that she stay all night, for she could never go all that distance before dark. Annie consented, but hardly knew how she could wait until morning to start on her journey. She rested and visited with the kind family, but went to bed early for she wanted to be up early in the morning to start home. She slept upstairs all alone in such a comfortable bed she dreamed all night long of running away from someone, and that she had made friends with a real Queen somewhere in her travels. In the morning she had to think hard to make herself believe the dream was not true. And little did she think that while she was yet young she would meet and make friends with Queen Victoria, and that she would receive presents from her.

In the morning when Annie was ready to start on her journey, she thanked the old neighbor for her hospitality and received the reply, "Lo me, child, why I would do anything I could for any of your mother's children, for hain't she done a lot for me? I hain't forgot when my Jim was almost dead with the fever how your mother sat up all night with me when I was afraid he wouldn't live 'til morning; my sakes, I'm glad to see you, and wish you would stay a week." Annie said, "Good-by," and started on her lonely way, for part of the road went through the woods. As she trudged along she had one fright when she met a man that frightened her almost out of her wits, but she ran and got away from him; and the remainder of the journey was without adventure.

4
THE RETURN HOME

WHEN SHE REACHED home she was joyfully greeted by her mother and sisters; and what a surprise, and how happy they all were! Emily, the half-sister, had called the new member of the family, "Grand Pap Shaw," so the whole family adopted the name for him. The mother could hardly believe Annie's story of how she had been treated while she had been with the farm family as their little drudge, but when they compared stories they knew things had been misrepresented to the mother, and that Annie had never been given a letter her mother, had written, for she had asked Annie to come home and had told her that she would have room for her and that she needed her to help care for Emily, the baby sister.

The mother was shocked when she asked Annie to tell her the story from the time she left the Eddingtons. The story was quickly told, and at the finish her mother arose, and with eyes ablaze exclaimed, "Those brutes! How did they dare!" By this time Annie was so glad to be with her mother she forgot some of the most brutal occurrences. But she told her mother she had been struck on the back while she was working as a little drudge. The mother looked at Annie's back, and as she did so she exclaimed with a low gasp, "My God, child, when did that happen?" And when Annie told her how long ago she had been struck, her mother suffered pain in her heart to see the poor little shoulders were still black and blue.

Annie told everyone her reason for coming home was that she could not stand to be away from her mother any longer. She was afraid the wolves would come and get her again if they heard she had been dissatisfied with them. Sure enough, they did try to force her to go back to their farm, but the Eddingtons made it clear to the cruel farmer that he would be in trouble if they ever tried to take her back.

The whole family was surprised to see how many things Annie could do, for she never hesitated to try anything the grown-ups could do. That night Annie's sleep was uninterrupted except for the dream she had of the old beech tree under which she sat slowly singing to sleep her curly-headed sister while she sang, "I have a Fazzer in de Plomised Land." Annie had often sat at the foot of the little crib and sung her sister to sleep. Her favorite song was, "I Have a Father in the Promised Land."

It did seem a little strange to Annie not to have the eldest sisters at home. Lyda,* the eldest of the family, had married Joseph Stein, a young carpenter, and was living in Cincinnati, Ohio; Sarah Ellen by this time was Mrs. Martain and also lived in Cincinnati; and Elizabeth had married a Mr. Brewer and lived even farther away, and it was a long time before Annie saw any of the older members of the family again.

Thus Annie was the eldest girl at home; but there was John, and Hulda, my mother, who had returned to her own people when she was about eight years old. Emily Brumbaugh, the half-sister, was as much a part of the family as any of the other children.

Annie's new stepfather, Grand Pap Shaw, had been a prosperous farmer and had plenty of stock and farm equipment, and owned a good farm of something like a hundred acres. Only a short while before he had married Annie's mother, his only child, a daughter, had married for the second time. Her second husband was a doctor who had recently come to the community. He was a smart, sleek fellow, and had persuaded Mr. Shaw to sell his farm and all of the equipment, and go to town and start in some business. Before the prosperous farmer got started in the business, the doctor had most of his money, by some hook or crook. However, Mr. Shaw did keep

* Lydia was also known as Lyda.

about five hundred dollars—enough to buy a small piece of ground with no buildings on it. There was plenty of timber on the land, so they could build a log house without costing so much. They built rather a modern one for that time.

When Mr. Shaw sold his farm and equipment, he kept as presents for Susan's children, a colt called Billy, for John; a riding horse they named Nelly, for Emily. Hulda seemed to like a calf for her pet, so he gave her a fine young heifer. The three children were delighted with the presents from Grand Pap Shaw, as all farm children love to have animals to call their very own. Annie was with the wolves about forty miles away from home at the time, and what he thought of for her I do not know. The two horses and young heifer were all a great help to the whole family later when the new house was completed and the family moved to the small farm that proved to be the happy home for them all that they had hoped for. Hulda was glad to be home with her family again, but never forgot the people who had been so kind to her during the years when her mother needed help most.

Grand Pap Shaw used Nellie part of the time to carry the mail from Greenville to New Weston, the nearest post office to the Shaw home, for he had kept the mail route, and that gave him a small regular income. When the log house was finished it was called a house, rather than a cabin, for there were two rooms downstairs, and two up. There was a small mortgage on the place, and it was a desperate struggle for them all to clear this home of debt, and make the house livable at the same time. Everyone was glad to do his part, for Grand Pap was a fine man, kindly and beloved by all. He was well read, too, for his time and place. He was considered by all who knew him to be a real gentleman, and a good Christian, and his opinion was valued by everyone in the community as being the best on almost any question. I remember hearing the whole family talk of the affection they had for the old gentleman, and years later when he grew old and blind they all felt a great sympathy for him, and a love that would have been unusual in his own children. Emily seemed to be the one closest to him, for I never heard her speak of him without tears in her eyes, she had so much sympathy for him in his blindness, and spent a great deal of time reading aloud the things he most enjoyed the last few years he lived.

On her return from the wolf farm, Annie fitted happily into the family again, and was, no doubt, very glad to forget the tragedy of the years behind her; but she never really forgot them to the end of her life. The horror of those two years with the wolves was burned into the sensitive child's mind, and left their mark upon her character. In later years when her success had come, helpless and neglected children found her purse always open, and whole Orphan Asylums along her route were guests of Annie Oakley.

This experience also had the immediate effect of maturing her beyond her years. An individual of ten, who had stood alone making her own decisions in what was for her a cruel and oppressive world, could not become a child again. A character naturally strong and dominant, asserted itself at home. She became one of the bread-winners of the family, as will be told presently, and her will began to clash with that of her brother, John, an unhappy condition that continued from that time on.

It was a childish thing that started it, but psychologically, that too, had its roots in the unhappiness of the wolf period. In how many ways the little girl suffered, we can only conjecture by its effects later; but the blow to her pride must have left a deeper mark than the blows on her body.

5
THE NAME CHANGED

THE CHILDREN AT SCHOOL, during the time she went to school for a few weeks from the wolf farm, ridiculed her name of Moses, and had made a hateful rhyme of it. "Moses Poses," they sang. And when she returned to her home she would no longer admit that the name of Moses belonged to her. Her mother had twice changed her name since Annie had been born, and the older girls were now married and had other names. Only John disputed it with her, and continued to hold his ground. Hulda did not like to argue, and refused to enter into the disagreement. But Annie asserted from then on, that the name was Mozee, and not Moses; and it appeared in all documents from that period. Her iron will is apparent here for she never admitted her name again. Some time later she destroyed the family record bearing the name Moses, and the family gravestones she herself had cut as she willed.

It was an odd obsession—understandable in a hurt little girl, but bewildering in the successful woman. Yet she clung to this all her life, and it is only recently that I, myself, have quite realized the cause of the family controversy which, of course, I knew existed, and that my dear aunt was utterly in the wrong. As long as my mother lived she never felt like taking sides in the argument, for to her harmony in the family was more important than a family name.

In spite of the life-long feud with John, the new home was a very happy one. The younger children went to school, and in due time Annie went for a visit with the Eddingtons, and of course she

35

told Mrs. Eddington all about the experience she had on the wolf farm, and said, "she wished she had gone home, or stayed with her good friends, instead of wasting two years."

Annie felt she wanted to help do some sewing for the poor children in the County Home, but the first thing she did was to make herself a dress that the Eddingtons had given her the material for. She did most of the sewing on her own dress by hand, for the sewing machine was out of order. Mrs. Eddington had examined the machine and decided it would have to be repaired before it could be used, because it dropped about every fourth or fifth stitch, but said, "We can cut and baste some garments until we can send for the Machine Agent to come out from Greenville to fix the old sewing machine."

Annie looked into the machine and found it full of lint. She threw the band, and turned the top back, and looked some more, then she said, "I think I can fix it." With an indulgent smile Mrs. Eddington said, "Why it takes an expert an hour or two to put a machine like that in shape," but she made no objection when the child began the machinist's task. The busy little hands worked for three hours, every part was taken off, cleaned and replaced. After that, the top plate, together with the gingerbread filigree sides of highly polished iron. The dust was taken out of the whole machine, and every part properly adjusted and oiled. Annie was pleasantly surprised when she ran a strip of muslin through to try the stitch, and it worked perfectly. Mrs. Eddington was delighted, for by Annie fixing the machine she had saved several days' time. There, was, of course, no telephone to step to, to call the agent, and no mail route so that she could slip a postal card into the mailbox and in a few hours let the agent know she would like the machine adjusted. It would have been a question of someone driving to town to tell the man there was a sewing machine that needed fixing at the Home.

Annie had earned two dollars, which she got for her expert work, and that was the start she had in saving money. Mrs. Eddington was so delighted too, with the sewing Annie did, that she asked her to stay a little longer and do some sewing that was so badly needed for the children in the Home, telling her that she would receive the same pay that any seamstress would have. Annie stayed long enough to make two dresses for each of the little girls in the Home, and how proud they were of the pretty calico home-made frocks their young friend had made for them.

Mrs. Eddington was so glad to pay Annie for her work, but best of all, she felt a great joy in her heart, for she had taught Annie how to sew and knew that her approval of anything Annie did was like dew from Heaven as it fell upon young grass that had been scorched and withered by the hot sun. In after years, when either temptation or discouragement was about to overtake Annie, she would look back to the time she had spent with the Eddingtons, and remembered what her good friend had said to her, "That some day she would be a great woman if she ever had half a chance."

Annie could think of many places to spend the money she had earned sewing for the children at the Home, but she had made up her mind to save for something most important, and that was to help pay off the mortgage on the family home. She decided then and there that if she ever earned money and spent it foolishly, she would see in her sleep the tear-stained faces of many little children, helpless and in need.

Back at home again, the only way Annie, as frail as she was, could think of earning enough money to help pay off this debt, was to turn to her skill of hunting and trapping again. This she did, and in a short time she was shooting more game than the family could use, so she went to Greenville to see if she could market the wild game that was so plentiful at that time. She went to a Mr. Ketzenberger, who kept a General Store, and who had always sold her the ammunition she used. He saw no reason why someone in Cincinnati would not be glad to buy the game, so he, through someone he knew in the city, found a Mr. Frost, a hotelkeeper, that was willing to buy Annie's supply of wild game. Mr. Frost used the meat on his tables in his dining room, and paid her a reasonable price. In this way she could save money toward the new home, and when eventually the last note was to be paid that gave her mother the clear deed to the farm, it was Annie who made the final sum that cleared the farm. She had earned it all by her clever shooting and trapping.

It was during these five years, from the age of ten to fifteen, that Annie for her own amusement began to do trick-shooting when alone in the woods. She dreamed of the time when she would become a champion shot, perhaps the champion of her own county, or to set her mark a little higher, the champion of her State. At that time her dream had never gone so far as to hope to be called the champion of the world, as she was called for so many years after she became better known than any other woman that lived during her time.

While Annie was engaged in marketing her game by sending it to Greenville by the mail carrier that carried the mail from the little town near her home to the County Seat, Hulda and Emily were busy felling trees and helping to clear a small spot of ground near the new house for a garden. Then came the orchard and the berry patch. It was Annie who bought the apple and pear trees for the young orchard. Apple blossoms had always been her favorite flower, and in later years she liked to be home with her mother when it was time for the apple trees to blossom.

At a very early age Hulda showed some talent for drawing and painting. Before she ever had money with which to buy paints, she used pokeberries and elderberry for coloring, and Annie was most encouraging and always tried to have her talented sister paint apple blossoms. She was so elated when Hulda was able to afford a small box of oil paints. To please Annie, Hulda was ambitious to be able to paint apple blossoms, rather than anything else. Eventually she must have accomplished this, for as a small child I can remember seeing sprays of apple blossoms on the parlor stand cover in my grandmother's home, and on a pillow that we were told not to lie upon, that graced the old-fashioned sofa. If anyone ever did risk taking a rest upon the sofa, they were supposed to take the velvet pillow off and put it on a chair. There was another pillow too, I especially remember, that had metal fringe around the edge that looked like gold. As the pillow began to age, my brother and I loved to have one of the strings of fringe fall off so we could unravel the metal that seemed to be like tightly twisted springs. Once the thing was unraveled there was no way to get it back in place, and more

than once I felt a sick feeling in my small tummy when my brother
had pulled a piece of the fringe off the pillow and unraveled it;
then we took it to the barn to hide our crime in the hay, or to the
cornfield to slip the handful of metal thread under a shock of corn,
All of this proves, of course, that by the time I was a small child,
the family had achieved the distinction of a properly furnished
parlor, and with not only comforts, but some degree of elegance.

Last of all, the little home was made complete when they had
built the up-ground cellar, or springhouse, as it was sometimes
called. Here they could keep the milk cool in summer, as well as
the apples and potatoes for winter use; and even well into the following summer.

At last Susan had a real home, and the family fortunes were
running smoothly. It was in this house Annie lived from the time
she was about ten until she was fifteen, when she went to visit her
sister who lived in Cincinnati. And to this old home she returned to
visit her mother, year after year when she was on the road, usually
after the late fall hunting season opened, sometimes staying all winter until time to return for the opening of Buffalo Bill's Wild West
Show. She seldom was able to stay at the old home late enough in the
spring to see the apple trees blossom, and that was always a regret.

In later years the house was improved from time to time with
the money Annie sent home for that purpose, and with the help of
my own father who remodeled the house to suit the one-time hard-
working Susan, whose life was free from hard work and care the
last years of her life, thanks to Annie's never-failing devotion and
affection. I remember the house well, for I often visited it later
and sometimes with my aunt. It still stands near North Star, a small
town in Darke County, Ohio.

My grandmother was a perfect housekeeper, and Annie's home,
which was also my mother's, is in my mind a very clean place. It
had in my time, in the main part of the house two rooms, one used
for a bedroom, the other a parlor; and to the back of the house
there was a frame kitchen and dining room, always painted inside
for the walls and ceilings were finished with a fine narrow board
they called "ceiling lumber."

The two bedrooms upstairs were furnished with the old beds the family had used for so many years, and were cord beds fitted with straw ticks and feather-beds on top, so the beds were so high, when we were small children we had to be helped into bed, and then we were always afraid of falling out, for we knew it was a long way down to the floor. The high chests of drawers were made of walnut, and looked to me as if they had been polished with oil, or something to make them shine; the chairs were not built for the comfort of small children either, so the only real fun we had going upstairs to sleep in grandmother's house was in climbing the narrow winding stairs that were different from the stairs we had at home. The stairs never had carpet on them, but as I remember they were scrubbed as white as wood could be made. Somehow there was always a certain thrill about going to bed in the high beds—they always smelled so fresh and clean, for in my time there was seldom anyone slept in the upstairs unless my mother took my brother and me for a visit.

The kitchen was the center of every household, and my grandmother's was no exception. There was a place in the new kitchen for the old iron pots and skillets, and the tin pans that were kept scoured as bright as a mirror with dust of a soft brick bat. What they called a scouring-box, had a place for the very finest brick dust, and that was used to scour the best steel knives and forks on the slanting board that was a part of the scouring-box. There was a place for the brick dust that had been pounded a little coarser, and it was used for the heavier iron pots and skillets, to keep them shining like new. The new tin pans were all hung on the wall near the kitchen stove that had the hearth scoured as bright as the cooking utensils. The old pot-bench was kept scoured with sand to make it as white as the floor in the sunny new kitchen, and there was a gay calico curtain to dress up the old bench, and it looked as attractive to the old-fashioned housekeeper as our fine new cabinet-sinks look to the modern housekeeper of today.

The new kitchen floor was never allowed to get dirty, for there was a regular day each week set aside for cleaning the kitchen, when all of the pots and pans had an extra touch with the brick dust, and a piece of old cloth, and when the floor was scrubbed with sand, for there was not much money for scouring material The soap that was used was made from discarded fat from the family's supply of meat. Susan had built what was called an "ash hopper," where ashes from hardwood were stored, then water was poured on top of the ashes and allowed to run through the ashes into a large stone jar, or an old iron kettle, and stored until there was enough lye to put with the fat; then it was boiled over an out-of-door fire in a big iron kettle until it was soft-soap. If they wanted the soap to be hard, they added a little salt and poured the soap into a wooden box lined with a piece of cloth, and let it stand to harden. The older the soap got, the stronger it was, and the better it was considered. The hard soap was usually used for washing dishes—it was a little more convenient to handle than the soft soap. A good many years after Susan could afford to buy soap for household use, she still made her own homemade soap, for she wanted to know what was used, and she said it was extravagant not to make the best of everything.

By the time Annie was fifteen the homestead was established and running smoothly, and it was then that her eldest sister, Lyda, and her husband (Mr. and Mrs. Joseph Stein) invited her to come visit them in Cincinnati where they lived, no doubt thinking that she had well earned the trip to the city. I can imagine how excited she must have been at the very prospect.

Her brother-in-law, of course, knew about her having shipped wild game to the best hotel in the city, and he happened to know Mr. Frost, the owner of the hotel. They both belonged to the same Gun Club, and at a regular Club Shoot Mr. Frost had taken one of his guests at the hotel, who was a good shot. When the trap-shooting for the day was finished, the guest had won, and Stein boastfully said, "That's nothing, I have a kid sister-in-law at my house that can beat the socks off that fellow." Mr. Frost was interested, and said, "Bring her out and we will have a match between them Thanksgiving Day." Mr. Frost knew who Annie was, but had never met her, but was willing to take a chance on the little country girl, and said he would put up fifty dollars in cash as the prize.

6

THE FIRST SHOOTING MATCH

THIS WAS THE FALL of 1875. Thanksgiving Day was chosen for the match (as was very customary at that time), which was arranged for the entertainment of the town people and hotel guests, as well as the members of the Cincinnati Gun Club.

A Stock Company had opened in the best theatre in Cincinnati, and the owners, Butler and Graham, did fancy shooting between the acts, for in those days it took some time to change scenery—they did not have the mechanical devices they now have for shifting the heavy sets. The two young men made a great hit with their fancy shooting and telling jokes on the townspeople. They were heralded as wonderful shots by the newspapers, and they were packing the house at every performance.

Butler and his partner, Billy Graham, were guests at the Frost Hotel, so Mr. Frost carelessly asked Mr. Butler if he cared to shoot a match at the Club on Thanksgiving Day. Shooting matches seemed to be the favorite sport for holidays. Butler asked, "With whom am I to shoot the match?" The manager's answer was, "Oh, someone from up in the country." Butler had asked if it might not be one of three shots well-known in that part of the country, and when he was told it was not, he remarked, "I won't mind picking up some extra money."

Annie had had the thrill of her life when she saw the city for the first time, and to be challenged to shoot a match with a theatrical performer almost overwhelmed her, but she was determined to win. The day of the shoot, the slender, shy little girl had her father's old Kentucky rifle all polished up for the occasion. She had made a new pink gingham dress to wear, with a sunbonnet to match. One can imagine how she must have looked with her blue-gray eyes sparkling with excitement, and her long chestnut hair braided and hanging down her back in two pigtails tied at the ends with narrow pink ribbon.

The shooting ground was some distance out north of Cincinnati, not far east of where the Cincinnati Northern railroad goes through from the north. My aunt has often pointed out the place where she shot her first match, for the spot held many pleasant memories for her.

When Annie and her sister and brother-in-law arrived at the shooting ground, Frank Butler and Mr. Frost were there. She was shy and did not dare to speak to them. The manager and two of the judges had just finished making the boundary line. Frank asked who the little country girl was that carried a gun. When he was told she was the girl with whom he was to shoot the match, he thought Frost had planned a joke, so he laughed and felt sure he would win the fifty dollar cash prize. Annie shot with her old muzzle-loader, but it was a good one, and they used two traps. Frank won the toss, and took his position at the traps first. The score kept even until the last clay pigeon he shot fell two feet beyond the boundary line. Annie had to score the last bird to win, and she did. He always said he let her win the match, and she would just blink her eyes and smile. She was a happy girl when the judges handed her the fifty dollars in cash as the prize. She had never earned so much money in so short a time before.

There had been a large crowd to watch the shooting match, and when Annie won the prize the people cheered until they were hoarse. When Frank left Annie and her family after the match, he gave them tickets to the theatre for the next week. They were going to play *Uncle Tom's Cabin*, and at that time Frank and his partner, Billy Graham, were doing fancy shooting stunts between the acts. Frank had a white French poodle dog named George that he used in the act. They did a William Tell stunt.

George would balance objects on his head, and his master would shoot them off. Sometimes he held an apple on his head, and when Frank shot the apple into pieces with a twenty-two rifle, George would jump with glee and catch the largest piece in his mouth and run to the front of the stage and lie down with the apple between his front paws, and wait for the audience to applaud. Then he would lie still and eat it. George disliked women so much that Frank was always watching him for fear he would bite any woman that might try to make friends with him; but he was a regular pal to Frank if there ever was one.

The big night came, and Annie and her sister and brother-in-law went to the theatre. This was the first real show Annie had ever seen, and she thought it all wonderful. When it came to Frank's act with George, the dog allowed his master to go through his act until he shot the apple off his head, then he caught the largest piece in his mouth and walked to the footlights, jumped over the orchestra pit and ran through the audience to where Annie sat. The snow-white dog then laid the piece of apple at her feet, put his head in her lap, and looked up at her with his big brown eyes. When Frank came through the audience, the dog growled at him as if to say, "I've found a friend, go away and let me be." By the time Frank got George back on the stage ready to finish the act, the scenery had been changed and the show was ready to go on. Frank made some funny remark, and the audience thought George had been trained to do the trick of jumping over the footlights and going out into the audience to find a girl for his master.

Frank had invited Annie and. her relatives to come back stage when the show was over, which they did, and George made friends with her. That was most unusual for he never liked a woman to come back stage, and would never allow a woman to touch him. Frank thought it strange that George should be friendly with Annie, so he got Mr. Stein tickets for the show for the next week. The show was to be East Lynn, and Frank and his partner were to do some shooting between acts as usual.

The night came when the three friends attended the show again, and somehow George knew they were there. When it was time for his act, this time he did not even wait for his master to shoot the apple off his head, but went to the front of the stage and before his master could get him, he was out into the audience looking for Annie. When he found her he put his head in her lap, and when Frank came for him he growled as if to say, "Let me alone, I'm happy here." This time they all laughed, and Mr. Stein invited Frank to dinner at his home, and he was to bring the dog with him.

Frank Butler decided that if George liked Annie he had made a good choice, and he began to see her. He took her to the theatre often, and she had her first dinner in a restaurant with him. They often had dinner in the Hotel with the Manager who had arranged their first Shooting Match. Frank and Annie's brother-in-law, Joseph Stein, became good friends and often met at the Gun Club.

Annie was always thinking of how she could help her family, and one of the things she did was to have her favorite sister, Hulda, come to visit with the sister in Cincinnati. When the sister and her husband found out how clever Hulda was with a needle, they arranged for her to stay long enough for her to learn the dressmaking trade. That proved to be a great help to her, as well as to the rest of the family. Mr. Stein was surprised to see how well Hulda could draw with a pencil, and he bought her a few tubes of oil paints. He and Lyda were delighted with the painting she did for them. She painted some scarves for the backs of their chairs, and a stand-cover or two, all made of velvet and lined with a different material.

When Hulda talked about her experience in the city with her sister and her husband, she always told of the happy time she had and of how hard she had tried to be a help to her sister. The only time she was ever corrected was one day when she was paring potatoes. Lyda thought she was peeling them too thick, and told her she was wasting the potatoes. Hulda had never known just how much her family had to economize, for she had been with the well-established prosperous family during the years when things were the hardest for her mother after her father died. Her sister Lyda had been taught to save everything she could, and Hulda was sorry she had to be corrected for anything.

After Hulda learned the dressmaking trade, she returned to her mother, seemingly quite an accomplished young lady, for she had been taught to draft patterns according to the measurements of anyone she wanted to sew for. She astonished her friends with her paintings; and all in all, Annie and her family were quite as proud of her as a family today would be of a girl graduating from college.

By this time the members of Annie's family who had met Frank Butler, liked him, but rather thought him a man of the world. When they learned he had no bad habits—for he never played cards, smoked nor drank—they liked him all the more. Annie's mother had been taught (as all Quaker folk were) that cards were for gambling purposes only, and that smoking was a sin, as well as the drinking of any kind of liquor. She in turn taught her children the same doctrine. She had also been taught that to go to a show was a sin. What would Susan think of marrying a daughter of hers to a man in the Show business?

Annie Oakley wearing medal presented to her by the Prince of Wales.

7
THE YOUNG COUPLE ARE MARRIED

HOWEVER, ANNIE AND FRANK decided the romance had gone far enough, and that something had to be done about breaking the news to her mother. They knew Annie's mother thought a great deal of Joseph Stein's opinion, so they decided to give him the task of telling her all about Frank. Annie's sister Lyda and her husband, Joseph, made a trip to the little farm about eighty miles north, to tell her mother about the man who wanted to marry her clever daughter, Annie.

After they arrived and looked over the fine little orchard that was the pride of everyone in the family, and had been shown how many chickens the old hens had hatched, they went in to dinner. After they started to eat, Annie's mother began to ask about the young man who had been paying so much attention to Annie. Joseph decided it was time to tell her Frank Butler wanted to marry her daughter, and it was by his persuasion that the little Quaker mother was won over to sanction the marriage. I know he must have started by telling her Frank had no bad habits, for that was the best way to tell her Frank was an ideal young man for her daughter to marry. Frank really did not even smoke or drink, and he could not see any fun in spending any time playing cards, as cards at that time were used mostly for gambling, and not as they are today as a game for amusement. Joseph knew Frank would not mind his telling Susan all about him, for certainly someone would have to do it before she would give her consent for her daughter to marry a strange young man.

Frank Butler's life as a child was quite as adventurous and colorful as Annie's. He was born in Ireland. When he was eight years old his father and mother left him with an aunt, because he was the eldest of the family and they thought two children were all they could manage when they came to America. They expected to send for Frank later, but before they could send for the lonesome little boy, he found he did not like living with his aunt who was not too good to him. So he made friends with the Captain of an old sailing vessel that was coming to America in 1863, and worked for his passage by paring potatoes and helping on the deck.

When he arrived in New York and found out what a big city it was, he hardly knew what to do. But somehow he managed to exist by begging and doing odd jobs such as helping on a milk-wagon. In those days the milk had to be dipped from a can into a pitcher or pail which the customers brought to the milk-cart; or sometimes the milkman would carry the milk to the customer's door in a small dipper. Frank was some help to the deliveryman because he could carry the milk into the house from the cart that was always drawn by a horse. All of the time the lonesome homesick boy hoped to save enough money to get out West where his family lived.

The ambitious boy sold papers, worked in a rooming house for a place to sleep, and he worked in a livery-stable part of the time. Somehow, Frank always had something to do to get along until he was old enough to learn the Glass-blowing Trade. Then he found he was not strong enough to continue in it. He had to be out-of-doors, so he worked on a fishing boat for two years until he was strong enough to work in the city again. Later he married and had one son and one daughter whom he loved; but somehow he could not get along with his wife, and they separated in time. Some time after that he was asked to do an act in an amateur show. He was clever in training dogs, so he got a troupe of dogs together and trained them. Everything seemed to go along all right until he added a new dog to the troupe. A fireman had given the dog to Frank, and when he had worked with the dog until he was well trained, he added him to his troupe to work in a theatre in Philadelphia. The theatre was next door to a firehouse, however, and the first night he used the new dog in the act, just as he had the dogs on the stage, and ready to start them in the act, the firebell rang. The new dog started at once to go to the fire, and the whole troupe followed. Needless to say, Frank had a difficult time gathering up his dogs and getting them back on the stage. The dog act was a good one, so Frank went on with it, but he gave back to the Fire Department the dog which had caused so much trouble.

After that Frank always had something to do on the stage. He was a clever shot, and when he met a young man by the name of William Graham, whom he liked, they tried out some trick-shooting that could be done on the stage. They went into vaudeville as the team, "Butler and Graham," and made good. So in a few years they worked in Stock Companies. And when I say "worked," I mean just that, for they put on a different show every week, and they had to spend all of their time either at study or rehearsals when they were not putting on a show for an audience. A little later they decided to try to own their own Company, which they did, and it was then Frank met Annie.

After Annie received her mother's approval of Frank as her husband, she began making herself some clothes for the wedding. Calico was the material she had usually used for the clothes she made for herself, but since she was to be married, her sister Lyda insisted she have gingham, at least. Annie had been such a great help to her sister, so Joseph, who was much interested in the coming event and too thought Annie should have new clothes, was willing to give Annie a little extra money to spend. Annie put all the extra stitches into the clothes that would make them look their very best, and when she was married on the 22nd day of June, 1876, she looked as dressed-up as any bride of that time who did not have a great deal of money to spend. One thing I know, she was as neat as possible, for everything she ever made was perfectly finished.

The wedding must have been very simple. I never heard my aunt or uncle speak of it, except that Uncle Frank would tease her by saying that when he married her she had only a gingham dress. So I have always thought she was married in a gingham dress, and the time of year and custom of the times make it very probable. Frank was as proud of her as he could be, for he thought her a very clever girl for sixteen. He was ten years older than she, and most likely appreciated her ability to do the things she could.

George, the trained dog Frank had had since he was a puppy, divided his affections with Annie so that Frank was always left to sit in a chair alone and George would go nearest to Annie to lie down when they were all together. When they walked along the street, George always was by Annie's side, as if to guard her. All the rest of his life, the faithful dog showed a marked affection for his mistress.

8
THE FIRST APPEARANCE IN PUBLIC

AFTER ANNIE AND FRANK were married she thought she would at last have time to go to school. She had just started to study when one night Frank's partner, Billy Graham, was suddenly taken ill. Frank and the Manager of the theatre were almost distracted to know what to do, for to close the theatre would have meant disaster. They had borrowed money to open the season, and everything had looked as if they would make good, but without Billy the show could not go on as it was.

The show must go on. Billy thought he could go on with his part of the performance, until the theatre was crowded and only a few minutes remained before the show was to start. What was to be done? Then Annie said she could not see the Manager give the ticket-money back, and that she could do Billy's act.

The woman who had charge of the costumes hurried to help Annie sew up the side-seams of Bill's costumes so she could wear them in the emergency, for Billy was a much larger person than the slight, small-boned figure that was going to swing into his act without even a rehearsal.

When the Manager announced that a non-professional young woman would assist in the act, there was a roar of applause. Besides just holding the objects for Frank to shoot at, she did every other shot as Billy had done. Frank took the first shot, and she the second, and they went through the act with only one miss. The last stunt was when she shot a cork from the bottom of a wine-glass which he held in his hand. The audience gave a verdict of success.

The next day the newspapers were more than kind in their criticism of Annie's first appearance as a fancy shot, and this was the beginning of a long successful career.

The first thing the next morning Annie and the seamstress in charge of costumes were off to the stores to buy material they needed to make her some costumes that really fitted her.

Annie continued in the act, and George, the faithful white poodle, worked with them, counting every shot until it was time for him to jump upon his velvet and satin-covered table and hold the apple between his silky ears. When the act was over he always walked to the front of the stage between his master and mistress, and made his bow to the audience.

Annie decided that if she were going to work with her husband, she should have a professional name. One reason for wanting to use a professional name was that her mother did not like the idea of her going before the public. And as long as Annie was in the show-business some of her family did not think it was "Christian-like" to belong to a show; although they never objected to taking all of this world's goods they could get that she left after her death.

Annie and Frank had a hard time deciding what her assumed name should be, and after several names were suggested they decided upon the name "Oakley." It was supposed to be a family name of several generations back. I have never believed this, myself, and have always thought she simply took a fancy to the name, and thought it sounded well with Annie. The name always seemed to suit her, because she stood alone in her profession and it was not a common name.

Annie and Frank closed a successful Season with not too much money, but at least they were not in debt, and she had been able to send her mother some money which helped to make life a little easier for her. After the season closed they signed a contract with the theatre to work another season; and during that time they were able to save some money. They always included George in their acts, for to people who knew them the team was not complete without the dog that seemed to enjoy working with them. Frank was clever in thinking of new tricks and jokes, as well as working up new shooting stunts.

Because of Frank's ability to think of new attractions there always seemed to be a demand for their work in both vaudeville and stock companies, because as they became better known everyone knew that no matter how often they saw the team of Butler and Oakley they were sure of a treat with something new in the line of entertainment.

During the next two seasons the team of Butler and Oakley played either vaudeville or stock companies, with many unusual and interesting experiences. They met all kinds of people—some were the fine old troupers of that generation, and some were not so fine, who tried to copy their shooting by deception. These imitators attempted to fake some of their most difficult shots, without much success. Some slipped a few shot into the brass shells which were supposed to be rifle-shells, so as to make the mark easier to hit. Some even tried to make a glass ball that when thrown into the air would travel a certain distance and then break of its own accord. But it was too difficult to gauge the exact moment when the gun must be fired to make it appear that the shot had broken the ball. Annie, however, would rather not do a trick at all if she could not do it honestly; and neither she nor Frank ever wanted to fool the public. Perhaps that was the reason they had such a long successful career.

One of the most interesting experiences they had during this time was in 1882 in St. Paul, Minnesota, when they met Chief Sitting Bull for the first time. When the old Indian Chief saw Annie shoot, he said she had been endowed with a power from on high, or she could never shoot as she did. Perhaps this was one of the reasons Sitting Bull liked Annie and wanted to adopt her into his Tribe. Another reason was that he had a daughter who died at the time of the Custer Massacre, who was the same age as Annie was at the time he met her, and he said Annie could go on taking the place his daughter had held in his heart. The young Indian girl had made her father the moccasins he wore in the Custer conflict, and they were among his prized possessions that he later willed to Annie. Up to the time Annie was adopted into the Sioux Tribe, Sitting Bull had mourned the death of his daughter, but he seemed to get some comfort out of knowing Annie and having her adopted into his Tribe.

When the Adoption Ceremony was performed, there was an interpreter present so that Annie and Frank could understand the whole thing. After Annie was a member of the Sioux Tribe, the Chief told her all about the struggle between the white man and the redskins, as he saw it, and of how the Indians had been driven from their God-given heritage into the Big Horn Basin where they were living upon broken promises. Annie felt a great deal of sympathy for the Indians, and felt that they had not always been treated right by the white man, and the Government-agents as well.

The old warrior called Annie, "Machin Chilla Wytonys Cecilia," meaning "My daughter Little Sure Shot." It was he who gave her the name of "Little Sure Shot," that was often used during her career. He always kept a photograph of Annie near him, and would stand in front of it and say nice things about her before he asked a favor of the gods.

Annie and Frank continued in stock companies, or in vaudeville, as the team of Butler and Oakley until the winter of 1880, when they signed a contract with the "Four-Paw and Sells Brothers Circus," that lasted four years. Shooting under canvas was rather difficult because they had to use small loads in the guns so as not to cause any damage to the circus equipment.

One thing Annie did enjoy was the fact she could do some horseback riding. One of the few pleasures she had when she was kept on the wolf farm was riding a horse; when she had to bring the cows from the pasture a long way from the barns she was allowed to ride a good horse, only because she could do the chores in less time than if she were to walk. Since that time she had had very little chance to ride horseback, until the Arena Director of the Four-Paw Show wondered if she might be able to shoot from a horse's back.

Frank had never seen Annie on a horse before, and he was astonished at her riding, as was the Arena Director of the Show. When they found out she was an expert horsewoman, they at once gave her a place on the program to do some horseback riding. She, herself, developed the idea of riding and shooting at the same time.

The Management was so delighted with her act, that they gave her a raise in salary that she welcomed, for it meant that she and Frank could add to their already growing bank account just a little faster.

They did not enjoy traveling with the Circus, for they had never lived under canvas before; but in later years they loved the out-of-doors and grew so accustomed to life under canvas that Frank's brother often said, "Why they have lived in a tent so long they don't know how to live in a house any more."

Making mostly one-day stands was again a hardship for them, because they traveled by train at night in day-coaches, and had very few comforts during the day. When the weather was wet, they had difficulty even keeping well. They did manage to get into a hotel or boarding house on Sunday, where they could get something good to eat and have some rest which they needed badly. However, they were glad to be able to add to their savings, and they knew something would present itself later which they would like better. Altogether the arrangements were not satisfactory, with traveling accommodations anything but comfortable.

When the Season closed in the fall of 1883, Annie and Frank were both pretty tired, so they took George and went to Ohio where they could have a good rest and visit her family. By this time Frank had become acquainted with most of the farm boys, as well as the men of the community. When they congregated in the General Store in North Star, the nearest town to the old home, Frank provided a great deal of entertainment for the townspeople. Some of the jokes he told were favorites in the community for years afterwards. Often when a good joke was told which Frank had not originated, someone would pipe up and say, "I bet that is one of Frank Butler's jokes." His funny stories were always clean, and safe for anyone to hear.

When the weather permitted, Annie and Frank both went hunting in the field with some of the country men, and their feats of shooting wild game were a source of interest to the whole community. By the time tales of their skill had been told several times, Annie and Frank often would not recognize them. Nevertheless they enjoyed seeing the neighbors have a good time even at their own expense.

Often in the evening Frank would walk to North Star, a mile away, and visit with the men who came in to sit around the old stove in Frank George's store. There was the row of barrels filled with crackers, sugar and salt, and even the old "spit tune" near the stove. The regular visitors enjoyed Frank's Irish wit and funny stories, while Annie stayed home with her family. She kept herself busy getting her clothes and costumes ready for the next season, for every year there were new things needed to complete her wardrobe. She never changed the style of her costumes after she began wearing the knee-length dresses. But there was always mending to do on the old costumes, for she would never wear a garment of any kind which needed the least bit of mending to put it in perfect condition. She never minded wearing the oldest clothes, if they had been made to look their best by either repairing or pressing. She looked after Frank's clothes in the same way she did her own, and it meant a lot of work—there were no dry-cleaners to keep clothing cleaned and mended, there was just the old-fashioned tailor, and sometimes he was not particular enough with his work to suit Annie. The busy little performer was willing to do a lot of extra work on their clothing in order to save money. She always considered she could either put the money she saved in her own growing bank account, or give it to some member of her family who had not had her opportunities for earning money. Often she was able to buy a piece of new material to send home to her sister, Hulda, to make up for herself or some other member of the family. She was always on the look-out for a new kind of material she felt she could afford, to surprise her mother or one of her sisters. Hulda usually did the dressmaking, and Annie was sure the material would be put to the very best use, even to the very last scrap, for her mother was waiting for every little bit of any kind of cloth that she could make into a comforter or quilt.

Annie and Frank helped to make the Christmas of 1883 the best Christmas her family had ever had; for outside of being able to give generously of gifts, they managed a shooting match for the amusement of the community. Everyone had so much fun that for many years people young and old told about the good time they all had at the Christmas Shoot. By this time Annie had several new guns which interested everyone who had not seen the most modern guns before, and she was generous enough to let several of the best shots try them out. Annie and Frank did some fancy shooting which greatly pleased everyone present, and the country boys ever after that were trying to do the same shots Annie had done, but most of them gave up in despair and were willing to admit it took a genius to do the kind of shooting they had seen Annie and Frank do.

The time was all too short, and soon the congenial couple had to go to the city to make ready for the opening of the circus. Early spring came, and they had to leave just as the trees in the apple orchard were beginning to show delicate pink buds, and again Annie said, "Oh, how I wish I could stay to see the apple trees in full bloom!" But they were off, and soon with Four-Paw and Sells Brothers' Circus for their fifth season.

Buffalo Bill. Thousands of these pictures were sold on the seats of the Wild West Show.

9

BUFFALO BILL SEES ANNIE SHOOT

AT THE VERY BEGINNING of the season they were playing in the South, for it was too cold for any circus to do good business in the North. It happened that the circus was in New Orleans at the same time Buffalo Bill's Wild West Show was there. The owners and partners of the Wild West Show were Col. William F. Cody (better known as "Buffalo Bill") and Nathan Salsbury (known as Nate). They, to be sociable with the Management of the Circus, as was customary, went to see the circus, and when Annie Oakley's act was called they were much interested. They had, of course, heard of the clever little woman who had been able to calm the warlike spirit of old Chief Sitting Bull, and who had astonished her audiences with her shooting skill.

Cody and Salsbury witnessed Annie's act with a great deal of interest, and as soon as her act was finished—even before the show was over, they went to the back of the arena to see if they could find her and tell her how much they had enjoyed the different feats she had performed with the gun and pistols. They were anxious, too, while both Shows were still in New Orleans, to impress Annie and Frank with the fact that they were with the wrong Company. They told the two famous shots that their act did not belong in a circus, but that it did belong in the Wild West Show which was trying to depict the life of the West, and in which all kinds of shooting helped to bring the western way of living to the East.

That very day the Manager of the Buffalo Bill Show made Annie and Frank an offer to bring their act to the Wild West, but they wanted more money to make the change than Cody and Salsbury wanted to pay. They endeavored to persuade them to accept less, but they would not. Finally Frank told the owners of the Wild West that he and Annie would work for their Show for three days at their own expense, and if they were not satisfied with their work, or did not think they were worth the money, the Butler and Oakley team would continue with the Circus. After three days' trial they never had to mention salary. Salsbury and Cody were more than satisfied with the act, and were convinced they needed Annie and Frank to make their organization complete.

The unusual couple went back to the Circus and asked for more money, but the Management thought they could not afford to pay it, and told them they knew they were worth more money if they could get it. So the contract with the Four-Paw and Sells Brothers' Circus was cancelled with the best of feeling existing between the Management and the performers.

When arrangements were completed between the Wild West Show and the team of Butler and Oakley, they naturally thought they would be asked to sign a contract. However, Cody and Salsbury told Frank that they had never had a contract with anyone, but that Cody insisted everyone's word should be as good as his bond and that if the people with the Show were treated right and fair, they did not need a piece of paper to keep them with the Show.

In March, 1884, Annie Oakley and Frank Butler joined the Buffalo Bill Wild West Show in Louisville, Kentucky. The day Salsbury and Cody introduced Annie and Frank to the Wild West company, was one they never forgot. When the people rode in from Parade, they were all ordered to line up. Annie and Frank rode up between the owners of the Show, and they were introduced as members of the company. The Indian Chiefs and their Tribes yelled, "Howe Waste," meaning, "All is good." Then the sound of a bugle was heard, and the entire company rushed under the friendly shelter of the big dining-tent, where many good things to eat were waiting for them.

At a feast such as this, it seemed they were all one big family. The owners of the Show were bountiful hosts at all times, and if there ever was a group of people well-fed it was the original Buffalo

Bill Wild West Show people. Annie and Frank always said the Outfit was more like a clan, than a business or a show.

At this time Frank knew the public demanded Annie all alone in her act as a shot and rider, and he, unselfish as he was, was willing to step out of the act as a performer and only assist her, as he was needed to put on the very best act he could produce for her. After the new act had been added to the Wild West, Frank became Annie's Manager and Director. He was anxious to have something entirely new, so they both worked a few days to complete new parts of the act, to have it go smoothly. They practiced in the morning, and in the afternoon after the show, when they could have the arena to themselves. The arena here was not covered with canvas as the one in the circus had been. It gave them more freedom, and they had an opportunity to do many different kinds of shooting, which they enjoyed.

After the act was completed, Salisbury came to Frank and asked for some photographs of Annie. He wanted tin-types, because he said they were best. He sent the photographs to a lithograph company in Hartford, Connecticut, and ordered three thousand dollars worth of printing, with the request that the order be rushed. The lithographs were three, six and nine-foot sheets. They were finished up quickly and used with the other advertising for the Wild West Show.

The lithographs of Annie used at that time were life-sized pictures of her riding a bicycle without holding the handlebars; riding around the arena holding a gun pointed upward, and shooting objects thrown into the air by someone on the ground. Another picture I remember was one of Annie standing upon a horse's back, shooting at glass balls thrown into the air by Frank who rode a horse by the side of hers. The printing used on this lithograph was "Little Sure Shot." Later the lithographs carried the title, "The Champion Shot of the World," but not until she had won the championship of France, and had won ever so many matches in America when challenged by champion shots of England. She never did like the title, but the Wild West's Advertising Man, Major John Burk, said she had won it, and so long as the Wild West Company was paying her the highest salary ever paid in the show business, they had a right to use the name, "The Champion Shot of the World."

Before Annie's act was a part of the Show's program, there had been but one solo act, and that was Buffalo Bill's, which was a good act, but he never did the different shooting that Annie did. After she came with the show, the program was made up entirely of cowboys roping wild steer, lassoing and throwing wild bronchos and branding them, as they did on the Western plains. I have even smelled the burning hair from the side of the struggling bronchos as the cowboys pressed the red-hot iron into the flesh of the animal to be branded. When I was a child and objected to this because I thought it cruel, Buffalo Bill said, "Why, that only makes the thing seem all the more realistic when the wind blows the smell of the burning flesh and hair into the audience that perhaps never would see the real branding done any other way."

When the old stagecoach rolled into the arena drawn by a six-horse team, the Indians followed closely behind. Soon the arena was filled with Indians and cowboys, whom Buffalo Bill had signaled to rush to the rescue of the stagecoach driver and his passengers, as well as to protect the United States Mail that was being carried in the stagecoach. Women were apt to shriek at the sudden gunfire when the cowboys began to fire at the Indians in the battle for the stagecoach. All of the program was as thrilling and filled with as much excitement as the two parts described, and it was a relief to see Buffalo Bill ride in on his beautiful, perfectly groomed, white horse, to do his shooting act all alone.

A girl alone in the arena was something no one had ever seen before, but after Annie did her shooting act, they were always more calm. They saw she handled a gun with as much ease as they did a knife and fork, and that there was very little danger in firearms as they were handled in the show.

Annie was the first and only white-woman to travel with a show like this, and society might have thought it impossible; but during the four years she was with Four-Paw and Sells Brothers' Circus, and the seventeen years she was with Buffalo Bill's Wild West Show, she proved herself to be a lady at all times, and shared the joys and sorrows of every member of the company. If any member of the company were ill or in trouble, he always felt free to go to Annie for help or advice, and many times she was a real comfort to one in sorrow.

Annie paid special attention to boys who ran away from home to join the show without letting their parents know where they were, and she saw to it that they wrote home. She often mailed the letters they had written, so she would be sure they were mailed. Many times she had letters from the boys' parents, telling how much they appreciated her seeing to it that the boys wrote home, and sometimes they came to see her personally.

Little Sure Shot, as the Indians called Annie, took a great interest in the Indians with the company, and taught them many things; and they all thought as Sitting Bull did, that she was a goddess, and said unless she had been endowed with a wonderful power she could not shoot as she did, so they had great respect for her judgment.

It was during the first year Annie was with the Wild West that Long John, the Pawnee, learned to trust Annie as he trusted no one else. He would not leave his money in the treasury wagon a minute after it was due him as his salary, but each week gave it to Annie to keep for him. But Long John liked to gamble when he had a chance. Once a Mexican, who was a rider with the Show, got John to shake dice with him. At first the Mexican allowed the Indian to win a small sum but when Long John began to lose and had to go to Annie for more money with which to gamble, he looked rather shamefaced. He asked for two dollars more of his money, then five, and then ten, and so on until his money was all gone. Annie warned Long John, but he would not listen, and would say, "No, Sistie, John bring back heap money." One morning after he had had his last dollar, Long John appeared in front of Annie's tent. His face looked troubled when she asked him if he came with heap money, he answered, "No, John heap fool." The truth was that the Mexican had used loaded dice, and John did not know it until after his money was all gone. John told the other Indians, and when they got the Mexican alone, they fixed him so he wasn't able to shake dice for a while. And John learned that what Annie told him about gambling was true; but the only way she could have taught him was to let him find out for himself, which he did, and he promised he would never gamble again. I can remember hearing my aunt say to John, "Heap much money, John?" And he would laugh, and say, "John not fool any more."

Even the roughest of the uneducated Indians seemed to change when they once knew Annie. The Management of the Wild West had always tried to keep the camp quiet and respectable, but at times had had a hard time managing because of so many people from rough canvasmen to the more refined performers, and officials of the company, to say nothing of the Indians and cowboys, and at least twenty-five band men, and the cook-house men that fed the people, over three hundred in all. Salsbury always said Annie had the power to do things he could not do, and he wondered if Sitting Bull were not right when he said Annie Oakley was endowed with a power from on high. It almost seemed so for if the roughest canvasman happened to swear in her presence, he would tip his hat and beg her pardon, and the cowboys were always most courteous to her. From the very first day Annie and Frank came into camp, every member of the company seemed to sense the fact they were entitled to everyone's respect, for they were all awed at the skill Annie displayed when she was in the arena, and she won the hearts of everyone with her grace and charm.

There was no menagerie, such as the Circus always had, but the people seemed to like to roam through the lot, and those who visited the Wild West camp found it almost as interesting as the Show itself, for they were allowed to roam through the camp at leisure, and watch the buffalo, Texas steer, elk, and the wild horses graze. They could walk through the long horse-tents where the draft horses were kept, and see them leisurely eating the best hay the Advance Agent for the Show could buy. The draft horses were used to draw the heavy wagons from the train to the Show grounds and back to the train when it was time for the Show to move from one town to another.

Visitors could touch the old prairie schooner, and even sit in the old Deadwood Stagecoach; and they could walk past the ammunition wagon and see how the glass balls were made which were used for Annie and Buffalo Bill to break by shooting them in their acts. One of the most interesting places in the camp was the cook-wagon, and the immense, dining tent. After the visitor had seen all of the Wild West camp, he had a fairly good idea how the big company lived under canvas. With so many people together, life went on very much the same as in a small town of the same size.

Visitors found many interesting people with the Show to talk to, although the show-people were not supposed to ever speak to the townspeople unless they were spoken to first, then they were allowed to answer questions and carry on a conversation. Everyone that came into the camp was watched by the Show's officers, although they were not aware of the fact. The company had their own police, the same as any small town would have, for it was necessary to keep law and order in the strictest sense of the word. Town toughs would often come to the show-ground looking for trouble; sometimes they would try to gamble with the show-boys, but Salsbury and Cody never allowed gambling if they knew of it.

The first year Annie and Frank were with the Wild West, they made nearly all one and two-day stands. Sometimes the trips were short, and the show could be loaded on the train after the performance in the afternoon, arrive in the new town in the evening and be unloaded by ten o'clock that night. Then the show-people could get plenty of rest, with the exception of the canvasmen who set up the tents, but they could get their needed sleep the next day. There was one performance a day at that time, but when they had all-night runs, it gave them little time for sleep because they traveled in day-coaches. In hot weather the canvasmen and some of the cowboys slept on the flat cars, underneath the big wagons loaded with the canvas and show equipment.

As she made a second trip to Europe.

10
MAKING A HOME IN A RAILROAD CAR

ANNIE AND FRANK had never had such luxury since they started traveling. The management of the big company wanted them to be as comfortable as possible, and had rebuilt one end of a coach so they could have a real bed, and a dresser and two comfortable chairs; they had running water in their state-room, and every convenience anyone could think of for the small space they had. Annie always had attractive curtains at the windows which matched the bedspread and dresser covers. It was their home for so many years, they were interested in having everything as nice as possible.

At the show-lot, they had a private tent. It was a center-pole tent, made especially for them, and it was set up at the end of the side-seats underneath the big top. That gave better protection from the weather, and also gave them more privacy, because the public was very curious to see Annie's guns and the medals she had won; and to talk with her gave many strange people a great deal of pleasure. She could not see everyone who wanted to talk with her after the show, so it was necessary to have her tent where she could be away from the people who wandered through the camp. Otherwise she could never have had any rest in camp.

In the private tent were her trunks, a table that was carried for writing, a hammock was fastened to the tentpoles so she could rest when she wished, and there was a good rug on the floor to make the tent more home-like. But for the comforts she had in the cozy little tent, many times she would have been inclined to give up traveling so that she might have the comforts of a home.

69

To hold the interest of the public, Salsbury was always looking for some new attraction to add to the already interesting company. He did not want it said that the show was always the same, so that people would not attend a second time; but rather, he wanted the public to attend his performances as often as possible to see what changes had been made. That was how he made a great success of a business which might otherwise have been a failure.

Salsbury always looked after the business-end of the Wild West Show. Cody was so good-hearted that he would loan any amount of money to anyone telling him a good hardluck story, and would never ask for security of any kind. He also enjoyed a good time, and would spend large sums of money showing a lot of people he was a "good sport" and a "good fellow." Consequently, he often would have had the Show in financial difficulties if it had not been for Salsbury, and that was the very thing that did happen after Salsbury died and Cody had to go on alone.

Before the close of the season of 1884, Salsbury was well satisfied with the dainty little girl and her shooting act, and so he began to search for something else to add to the program. Annie and Frank told him they thought old Chief Sitting Bull would be a great addition to the company. Both Salsbury and Cody liked the idea, and at once decided to try to see him. Pawnee Bill was then the agent with the Show who made arrangements with the Government to have the Indians travel. Pawnee Bill was sent by Salsbury to try to find the old warrior. After some time he found the old Chief and tried to persuade him to go East and join the Wild West Show, but for three days the Chief's answer was always the same, and all he would say was, "Sheeta," meaning, "No Good."

At last Pawnee Bill and the interpreter had an idea. They had noticed that several of the Indians who wished a favor granted by Te Tonka Ua Toka (Sitting Bull), before asking for the same would stand in front of a cabinet photograph of Wastanwa Cecilia (Annie Oakley) and say nice things about the photograph. They would ask questions about Sitting Bull's meeting with Annie in St. Paul in 1883, they would inquire about all the details covering the adoption, and ask his reason for wanting to adopt Annie into his Tribe to take the place of his daughter whom he lost at the time of the Custer Massacre. The reason was that Sitting Bull thought Annie felt he had fought justly, and that the little band of redskins had been slowly pushed into the Basin of the Big Horn where they could easily be annihilated. Annie said, "The lives that were lost then might have had a better ending."

The interpreter called Sitting Bull's attention to the photograph of Annie which the Chief prized so highly, and said to him, "Would you go East and join the Wild West if you could see Watanwa Cecilia?" He laughed and said, "Washstay." We would say, "O. K." Within an hour the old warrior had picked his braves and was ready. The interpreter was the same man who had been present at the time Annie was adopted into the Sioux Tribe in St. Paul in 1882.

When the Indians from the Sioux Tribe entered the Wild West camp, Sitting Bull was delighted to see Annie. After he had seen her act for the first time he decided the name he gave her at the time of her adoption into his Tribe was a good one, so he continued to call her "Machin Chilla Wytonya Cecilia" (My daughter Little Sure Shot).

After the Sioux Indians had been with the Show for awhile, Sitting Bull felt inclined to go on the War-path about something that happened which displeased him. Annie calmed him by simply talking to him and doing her queer little dance and step she did as she left the arena following her act; he laughed and was soon over the rage he had been in. After that, when the Chief started sulking as if he intended to start on the war-path, someone would call Annie and she would soon have him good-natured. One of the things the Chief liked to do, was to put on a pair of overalls and pound on tent-pegs. These were the heavy, short pegs to which the big tent's guy-ropes were fastened. I do not know whether he thought he was becoming civilized by wearing the overalls and working with the white man, or whether he simply wanted to show his strength; but I rather believe it was the latter, for if the townspeople chanced to stop to watch him, he would hammer all the faster. He loved dirty jewelry, and wore all he could find, and was delighted if anyone gave him anything he could wear around his neck. He was

supposed to have the best headdress of any of the Chiefs with the
Show, and was highly insulted if any of the show-people thought
he did not have the longest feathers in his headdress of any Indian
they ever knew.

One morning when the Show, arrived in Pittsburgh, a stranger
was waiting to see Sitting Bull. He missed seeing him at the train,
and by the time the stranger got to the show-lot the Indian tepees
were set up, and he hurried to find the old warrior. As he went
through the lot he kept saying, "Show the old renegade to me. He
killed my brother in the Custer Massacre. Where is he?" As the
stranger got near to Sitting Bull who was pounding at a tent-peg,
he tightly gripped the handle of his six-shooter and with an oath
told the Chief what he intended to do. Sitting Bull saw the six-
shooter pointed at him, and with his keen mind sensed what was
going to happen. He shifted his position enough to let the heavy
sledge he was using to pound pegs, go flying backward over his
head, and in an instant it had struck his would-be slayer and he
fell to the ground like a flash. The cowboys picked up the injured
man and laid him on a bale of hay. Upon examination it was found
that the stranger was minus three teeth and had a badly bruised
head. After a time he gathered his senses together and made his
way out of camp. Sitting Bull picked up the heavy sledge and slowly
walked into his tepee, closing the flap after him.

When Sitting Bull sat in front of his tepee after the show, if a
stranger walked past and spoke to him, he would nod his head and
say, "Howe." He wore his headdress most of the time, and carried
his peace-pipe, and liked to display his large bow with a sack of
his finest arrows which he had carried for many years in quest
of deer, panther, bobcat, elk and buffalo. When the Show closed
that fall, the Chief gave his prized possessions to Annie for safe-
keeping.

Next to Sitting Bull's tepee at the rear of the Wild West arena,
was the tepee belonging to Chief Geronimo, the Apache, who was
an entirely different type. Geronimo plundered and tortured, for
the sake of witnessing human suffering, and was difficult to manage in the performance of the Show, but he added interest to the

Indian Tribes because he was such a fierce-looking individual, and had so many scars on his face from fights he had been in.

The last two weeks of the Season of 1884 for the Buffalo Bill Wild West Show were spent in the rain—it rained continually. It was no wonder Annie was glad to hear the band play, as it always did on the last day of the season, "Should old acquaintance be forgot;" and the last familiar tune was always "Home Sweet Home."

During that Season Annie and Frank enjoyed what they thought to be the best time of their lives until then; they had saved money, and had kept well, and made many life-long friends. Thomas Edison, as well as Mark Twain, had been frequent visitors in the camp and made friends with Annie and Frank and Col. Cody and others. After the afternoon show the famous people often visited and enjoyed tea and sometimes did some shooting in the Arena. There had been many fine people with the Wild West whom they enjoyed, and they had met scores of people in their travels who became their fast friends. Some of the men who traveled with the Show those first years, became leading businessmen in different parts of the country. One man I remember knowing a good many years afterward, was in the piano business in Allentown, Pennsylvania; another, was owner and manager of a large hotel in Newark, New Jersey; still another was one of the leading advertising men in New York City, and many of them gave up traveling for one reason or another to go into some permanent business.

Annie and Frank with George, the French Poodle,
after he figured in the Romance.

11
GEORGE DIES

THE ONLY THING that happened to mar Annie and Frank's happiness, was the loss of their snow-white French poodle, George, that they had loved like a child. It was the spring, soon after they joined the Wild West, that George died. One night in a downpour of rain, Annie and Frank and George had made their way from the show-lot to the train, and the dog got so wet he chilled. They wiped him with bath-towels as dry as they could, but he took cold, developed pneumonia and died. It was a sad day in Camp when the news was spread that George was dead. The company carpenter made a wooden box and lined it with cloth. They wrapped George in the satin and velvet table-cover that had been used in his act, and placed him in the box, and two cowboys carried him to the grave that had been made in the beautiful lawn of a friend in Cleveland, Ohio. The Indian girls made wreaths of flowers and carried them to the grave, and they chanted an Indian hymn as the little box was lowered into the grave.

It was hard for Annie and Frank to give George up for he had been such a true friend, and as long as they lived they never forgot how he had played cupid in such a mysterious way, so his memory lived on and on. When I was old enough to remember the interesting stories Annie and Frank told when they came home, the story of George was one I loved to hear, and to see his picture made my heart leap with excitement, for the beautiful dog had been so real to me I even loved his memory.

The busy couple went on through the season without the dog in the act, and when fall came they went to Ohio, and all the family missed George too, because Frank had never visited them without his faithful friend; and this time they were made sad because Frank was lost without the dog that had been his constant companion for so long. There had been some sad changes in Annie's family too, and she was anxious to get home for a visit and to hear the story from her mother, whom she had always tried to comfort. By this time the two older sisters had died—the oldest one, Elizabeth, a widow, was tubercular, and came home to visit, but in only three weeks passed to the Heavenly home to join other members of the family. Lyda, the sister with whom Annie had visited in Cincinnati when she met Frank, contracted the same deadly disease, and in a few weeks died without ever having seen Annie work in the Wild West, though she knew of the success she had made.

Hulda, in appreciation of the help Lyda and her good husband had given her when they took her to the city so she could learn the dress-making trade, went to take care of the patient sufferer during the last months she lived. In a letter to a friend, Annie told of the death of her sister, Lyda, describing how her favorite sister, Hulda, was with Lyda at the last, and that "through the open window entwined with honey-suckle the gentle spirit caught a glimpse of something worth while, and started up the little path that led to the open gates of 'God's great world.'"

Joseph, Lyda's husband, as long as Annie's mother lived, visited her, and was on friendly terms with all of the members of her family. In turn they all had a great regard for him, and felt it was a great tragedy to lose such a congenial companion when he was so young.

Hulda helped Joseph Stein adjust his household as best she could after the death of her sister, then went home to rest, and to make herself a pretty dress of material Annie had sent her, and on the first day of March, 1884, Hulda Moses changed her name to Mrs. Stephen Shaner, and was happy in a home of her own. Hulda had earned all of the happiness that could come her way, for she too had worked all of her life to make the best of things, and to help to establish the family home as it was then.

The same day Hulda was married, her brother, John, was married to Laura York, a good friend of the whole family. The two new members were a great help in cheering the saddened family. Laura was of a cheerful disposition, and always saw a silver lining to every dark cloud.

Emily was now the only one at home to help her mother with blind Grand Pap Shaw. She always said it was such a pleasure to care for him because he was so patient, and tried to be as cheerful as he could through all of his illness.

Annie and Frank enjoyed their stay in the country, and were the means of some of the farm people of the community having two or three good shooting matches. They gave one exhibition which pleased the young shots very much; they had never even dreamed of such difficult shots as Annie and Frank showed them how to do.

Again it was time to think of planting some more fruit trees or berry bushes, and Annie helped decide what should be planted. Nothing seemed to give Annie's mother quite so much pleasure as to have a new kind of bush or tree to plant in the spring. The orchard and garden were the pride of the whole family. The mother worked in the garden as most farm-women did, and seldom could a weed be found there. The paths through the vegetable garden were usually edged with different kinds of lettuce, and there was always more than could be used on the table, but there were the chickens that could consume a great deal, and if there was more than they could eat, the pigs in the pen could eat any amount of any vegetable. Susan prided herself on being able to throw-up the high beds early in the spring, with the paths as straight as a line could stretch, and the lettuce kept the edges from being washed down into the paths by the rains.

The garden was on the hillside just south of the house, and it was the first spot of ground to dry out enough to plant in the spring, so they usually had vegetables before anyone else. At that time early vegetables were very welcome, for one could not buy shipped-in or storage fruit and green vegetables.

This particular spring Annie and her family found a new species of goose-berry, which was larger than any they had ever seen, so they bought some new plants to try. Every year or so Annie liked to buy something new that had not been grown in the neighborhood, because it gave her mother so much pleasure to show her prize fruit to her friends. Well I remember as a small child when I went with my mother or my aunt to visit grandmother, about the first thing we did after we arrived and had had a very short visit, was to go to the garden to inspect the growing beds of everything that could be grown in that climate. Grandmother was most generous with what she had, and if anyone was ill, or did not have the things she raised early, she divided with them.

The early spring brought regrets again when Annie and Frank left for the opening of the 1885 Season of the Buffalo Bill Wild West Show in St. Louis. They were in that city for a two-weeks run, after which they settled down to the regular routine, and played most of the big cities in the East. In Philadelphia a few guests were invited to the Wild West Camp to enjoy an Indian rib-roast. Sides of the best beef were barbecued over heaps of wood-coals, then cut into chunks and passed around in tin basins. The guests were given sharp hard-wood sticks, and were told to eat with their fingers. The meat was so good they ate until the last bite was gone. After feasts of this kind, great frolics took place which the guests always remembered.

Upon one occasion a bald-headed man asked Chief Geronimo, the Apache, if he could scalp a head like that, pointing to his own. The Chief had boasted that he had scalped more white men than any other Indian traveling with the Show, and seemed to be proud of the fact.

12
MARK TWAIN'S SUGGESTION

IT WAS AT ONE of these feasts Mark Twain suggested that Salsbury and Cody take the Show to Europe. For one thing, he said, it had been known that none of the exhibitions sent abroad had ever been strictly American; and, he said, "To the smallest detail the Wild West Show is original and strictly American." Mr. Clemens (Mark Twain) was a close friend of Buffalo Bill's, and frequently visited the Wild West Camp. He always enjoyed the performance, no matter how often he saw it. Mr. Clemens especially enjoyed the Wild West when they were in Madison Square Gardens in New York City, as they were for many years during the month of March or April. During a performance in the Gardens in 1908, I was talking with the famous humorist, and as my aunt came into the box where we were, he said to me, "Annie Oakley could hit anything with a gun that anyone else could, and then some."

During the first and second years that Annie and Frank were with the Wild West Show, so much had been said about the Show that P. T. Barnum came to see the performance. His comment was, "They do not need spangles to make it a real show." It was unusual for P. T. Barnum to go see any other Show than his own, which was strictly a circus.

After playing through the East, the Show went to Erskine, Staten Island, for the remainder of the season. There was to be a parade in New York City, and it was to be Annie's first parade in the great metropolis, so she wanted to look her very best. She carefully planned and fitted a pretty riding habit made out of light tan broadcloth to look like buck skin. She had everything to match, and even had the vocaroes with the name "Oakley" on both sides. Her outfit had cost a large sum for those days, and she had worked ever so hard to complete the whole thing in time for the parade to which she had looked forward for a long time. However, only a few days before the parade was to take place, an insect found its way into her ear, causing an infection and a high temperature, and the day of the parade she was told by the physician with the Wild West that she must stay in bed. But when Annie heard the band start playing "Marching Through Georgia," it was too much for her to stay in Camp when the parade had started for New York. She was so ill it took her longer to dress than usual, but while she dressed the groom saddled her horse, and she handed him her new vocaroes and was soon off. But it was not until the last of the parade had rounded out of sight half a mile away that she flew through the gates on her little horse. She made the ferry just in time to cross with the parade. She rested while she was on the boat, and was able to go through the streets of New York with the rest of the company. The parade was to be seventeen miles long, and there were thousands of people standing on the streets to witness the Wild West Parade. When the cavalcade finally returned to the Ferry, Annie was a limp little figure, and had to be lifted from her horse and put into a carriage for the remainder of the trip back to the Staten Island Camp. She was so ill she missed four days' work, and it was the only time she ever missed an appointment in over forty years that she shot before the public. However, she recovered finally and was soon back in the ring. She always said that, "By a merciful providence she had been spared the most dangerous form of blood poisoning."

At Erskine they were extremely popular, and successful. Twenty thousand seats had been erected to accommodate the people which seventeen steamboats took over from New York City for every performance. Members of the company made many life-long friends while there on the Island, and the Management realized a good profit, for the business had never been better for so long a period of time.

It was while they were on Staten Island that Annie and Frank had a chance to keep house for the first time. They had a small furnished apartment, and later she talked to me of her housekeeping experiences much as any young bride would. It was during the stay on the Island, also, that Annie was challenged by some of the best shots in the East to shoot for money and prizes.

It was then that she and Frank learned much about guns and ammunition, and she had some new guns made for herself. She used a number six soft shot, as chilled shot would have glanced off from the hard-clay pigeons they used at that time. Powder played an important part, also. If the pressure of the powder was too great, the powder was crushed and the load would scatter and not shoot true. The first smokeless powder they used would not work in brass shells, so they used black powder. At that time there was only one kind of clay pigeons. They were made of red clay, and some of them were burned as hard as stone, making it extremely difficult to break them unless they were hit exactly right.

Annie used a double-barrel, twelve-gauge gun for trap-shooting, but for some of her fancy shooting she used a rifle re-bored for shot, but used brass shells. She found that the shells they loaded themselves were less apt to be affected by the weather and the different climates, so they usually had the shells loaded in the ammunition wagon in the Wild West camp.

Besides her performance six days a week with the Show, her housekeeping, and doing a little sewing for herself, Annie found time to shoot some Matches. During the late fall and early winter she shot several matches and won almost all of them. She shot in and around New York, several places in New Jersey, and in Philadelphia.

One challenger, after the close of the Wild West season in September, was an Englishman who had come over to win the Championship of America. He had met in matches with several of the best Shots, and had won every match except one—a good shooter who had succeeded in tying with him. The challenge he issued to Annie was the best two out of three matches.

The first match was at Old Point, New Jersey. Annie did some practicing and felt confident she could win. The race was fifty birds each (one hundred to a side). The morning before the match was to take place, Annie shot twenty-five targets; then she asked Frank to try one with a new gun she had just received. He took the gun and stepped to the trap to try the sight to see if he thought it would shoot true. Annie slid a target into the trap and was withdrawing her hand when, z-i-n-g!—the spiral-spring, which was used in the traps in those days, flew out releasing the trap. The spring struck between her first and second fingers, splitting her hand open about two and a half inches. Luckily it struck between the bones.

The doctor forbade her to use her hand for at least two weeks, but Annie, with her usual determination, decided she would try, for she knew she still had two chances to win if she lost the first out of the three. The Englishman was glad she decided to try, for he felt more sure than ever he could win.

At nine-thirty in the morning of the day of the Match, ropes were stretched around the target-ground to keep people from crowding in where they would be in danger. There was a large crowd to witness the match, for the people who were interested in seeing the Champion of England shoot against the only American markswoman, were there. The time was announced, and Frank told the audience about the bad accident to Annie's hand, and stated that should she at any time during the match decide she could not finish the shoot, that the spectators might have the price of their tickets returned. He added, "If anyone is not satisfied, they can go now to the gates and get their entrance fee back at once." No one stirred. It looked as if it was going to be a more exciting match than they had expected, with the American favorite using only one hand.

Annie won the toss, and went to the traps. It was to be a live-bird match, and the birds were fast, but ran pretty even. Annie used only her right hand, keeping her left one in a sling. They both grassed the birds clean, up to the eleventh; then Annie drew a high-climbing, left-quarter, incoming bird like a streak of lightening. Her first barrel cut all of the tail-feathers off the bird, then she had to risk her left hand or lose the bird, because her gun was too heavy for a second one-hand shot. With her left hand she grasped the barrel of her gun, covering the bird with a clean kill, only to see it fall less than twenty inches over the boundary line. Three of the five stitches in her hand had been ripped out, and though she tried to keep the blood from showing, it trickled down from her elbow. Frank at once rapped upon the table by the Referee and announced that Annie would give the match to the opponent. The Englishman stepped to the trap for his eleventh bird, and he drew a ground-skimming, straight-away, which he missed clean with both barrels—and that meant a draw. Annie retired amid cheers. One spectator said he had had his money's worth seeing Annie shoot ten straight with one hand. Everyone thought they had their money's worth for no one went to the gates to claim his ticket-money. The last two matches were postponed until a later date, for Annie had won the match according to the number of shots fired.

Annie's hand was slow in healing, and it was after the first of the year, 1885, before she could do any more shooting. She then gave an exhibition at the Middlesex Gun Club at Dunellen, New Jersey. The Club members thought they would have some fun with Annie, so they used the strongest spring they had for the clay pigeon traps, and fastened it in the fourth notch in the arm that held the clays. Annie, thinking she might have a strong wind that day, had armed herself with some heavy shells, so she only laughed when the two try-out birds left the traps. After her rifle and revolver shooting, she shot at fifty clay pigeons, first single and then double. They threw two from the traps at one time; she shot one, then turned around and broke the other. She then did some other stunts. The last two shots she sprang the traps herself, ran twenty feet, leaped over a table, picked up her gun from the ground, and broke the two birds. Her score was forty-nine out of fifty, and the Club presented her with a handsome solid-gold medal.

At the Club that day they finished with a match between the two best shots in the Club. The honors were left to Annie and a one-armed New Jersey Champion—they shot it out together, and she carried the honors and money back to New York that evening.

As usual, the greater part of the prize money went to her mother in Ohio, to help make her a little more comfortable. The first time

Annie ever won a sum of money at a shooting match, she promised herself that every time she won a sum of money at a match she would share it with her mother, and she kept her promise as long as her mother lived. After her mother was gone, she gave it to charity—usually to help some under-privileged child.

Annie and Frank were well satisfied with their Season, and went for their annual visit to Ohio, to stay until the next spring when, for the first time, the Show was to open in Madison Square Gardens, New York; and the Management were very busy making ready for a bigger and better Wild West Show than ever before.

Annie did some studying, while Frank kept busy hunting quail, rabbit and squirrel. They spent part of the time on a farm with her sister Hulda and her husband, where Frank could hunt and try out a new dog which had been given to him. Because Frank had always had a dog, after George died some kind friend decided to give Frank a fine dog. Frank never liked the dog too well, but thought it would be a good time to try-out, and train the new animal, while he was hunting, so he took him along.

One day Hulda baked a pan of sugar-cookies, and left them on the bench under the windmill to cool, just about the time Frank brought the dog in from hunting. No one happened to be watching, and the dog climbed up and ate nearly all of the warm cookies. Frank said disgustedly, "A dog with no better manners than that should be chasing cows," and so he gave him to a farmer who needed a dog.

The old neighbors had not forgotten Annie, for there had been a great deal of talk about Annie Moses going to the city, shooting a match with a theatrical man and later marrying him. Annie and Frank took their guns with them, and did some fancy shooting for the pleasure of the old friends. Frank made friends with some of the farmers, and went hunting with them. In the evenings neighbors dressed in their best came in to visit with the little country girl and her husband. They wanted to hear about the shooting matches they had won, and all about their travels for in all the country there was no one who had traveled as much as Annie.

Some of the more sedate country men at first were of the opinion Annie had lowered her principles in having traveled with a

Show, but after they became acquainted with Frank, they changed their minds. They liked him, and his Irish wit, which afforded them a great deal of pleasure. He also wrote some poetry for them, which pleased them. The verse he wrote and left with them on this particular trip was, "Miss April."

MISS APRIL

How do you do, Miss April?
I'm mighty glad that you are here.
Never did like old, Miss March;
She acts so very queer.

Sometimes she smiles, and sometimes shines;
Next day she's cross and vexed.
She's just like some folks that I know;
Can't tell what they'll do next.

Miss March, Why do you act so mean?
You send your warming rain,
You start the song-birds from the South,
Then drive them back again.

Now, if somehow the pleasant task
Of naming months were mine,
March would be "Miss Blizzard,"
And April, "Miss Sunshine."

So many pleasant days were spent visiting old friends and Annie's family, that the winter of 1886 and 1887 was very pleasant and over much too soon. There still were things Annie wished to do, and most of all she wanted to stay long enough to again see the growing apple trees blossom, but time came to leave for New York to make ready for the big opening of the Show. This was to be Annie's first appearance before a New York audience.

Nate Salsbury, first manager and part owner of Buffalo Bills Wild West Show, taken in England before his tent.

13
IN MADISON SQUARE GARDEN

IT WAS THE SPRING of 1887, and the third season for Annie and Frank with the Wild West. A number of additions and changes had been made for the Season. The roof of Madison Square Gardens had been raised twenty-five feet or more, to make room for the vast scenery of the great indoor-pageant called, "The Pageant of Civilization."

A man named Nelson Waldron had invented a machine which produced cyclone effects. The stagecoach driver and passengers were blown off their seats as they drove through the mining town and the machine produced enough wind to even blow mining shacks down. Nate Salsbury saw to it he had some new acts which would open the eyes of everyone coming to see the Show. He had added some cowgirls to the troupe of roughriders. Frank had devoted enough time the Season before to teach Johnny Baker to shoot, and he now did a solo act which was cheered by all.

While the Company was in Madison Square Garden, Annie, too, showed the audiences some new stunts. One was sliding head-down from her saddle and untying a handkerchief from the pastern joint of her horse while going at full speed. And in the same position, picking up handkerchiefs and her whip. Each Monday night while they were in the Garden, Annie managed to add a new stunt to her act. The Management learned that people came every Monday night just to see what the new part of Annie's act was. She had not forgotten her first lessons in riding as a little girl on the wolf farm, but she had added to her experience in handling a horse by constant practice, until she was considered an expert horsewoman.

87

All of the new acts worked into the performance well, and the Show played to vast audiences the month it was in Madison Square Garden. It was during this period that Mark Twain saw the Show several times, and on each occasion told Cody all Europe would go wild over the Show, and that there would be nothing to worry about, insofar as attendance by the European people was concerned. After Mark Twain had so many times told Cody how much the European people would like the Show, Salsbury became keenly interested in taking the Show abroad. They talked about it until in a short time it became a reality, and they began making plans to do what seemed an almost impossibility, because to take the entire outfit abroad would alone cost over a hundred and fifty thousand dollars.

Annie, never forgetting her experience as a child, was always on the lookout for something to do for a poor child, or a group of children. So she asked Cody if she might not invite all the orphan children in New York City to the Show. Cody, ever generous as he was, consented to her having the Garden for one performance. There were hundreds of children made happy that day. Annie bought ice cream for all of her guests, and she, too, was as happy as she could be, because she had discovered a means of giving so many poor little children one of the most enjoyable days they had ever known.

Annie's Children's Day at the Garden proved to be one of the best advertising schemes they had ever had, although she had not thought of it in that light. Everyone around town was talking about Cody's generous gift to the children, and trying to figure how much ice cream Annie bought for her guests. Major Burk (who was the clever Advertising Man of the Wild West), often told about Annie's clever stunt, and laughed, saying that Annie had tried to compete with him in the advertising game. She was quite capable of doing so, too.

During this stay in the Garden, though it was March they had a big snowstorm, and Annie decided she would like to take a sleigh-ride around several blocks. So she had Old Jerry, the big, tame moose, hitched to the sleigh. They had gone but a short distance when Jerry saw a pushcart filled with red apples. It required only about three of his long strides for him to reach the cart, and push it over. The apples flew in all directions, and Jerry calmly ate as many as he could dig out of the snow. Annie paid the vender five dollars for the apples Jerry had wasted and eaten, and charged it to "advertising." The newspapers carried an article telling all about the trouble Jerry, the moose, had caused, and included a picture of him and one of Annie. And many people asked to see the moose when they came to the Show.

The Garden had been fixed for the convenience of the Wild West People, to the extent that it seemed almost as if the whole world were shut out. There were stores of different kinds, tailor shops, bootblacks in each corner, as well as newspaper stands, so they could buy almost anything they needed without going out of the building. The cook outfit was set up just as if they were on the road, and the entire company was fed without the bother of walking more than the length of the Garden. The whole place seemed like a town in itself.

The Management, at the time, was putting on the finishing touches in preparation for the trip to Europe. It all meant a great deal of work because they were to be gone for at least a year, and with so many people to arrange for, it was no small job. The Indians had never been taken out of the country before, and special arrangements had to be made with the Government for permission to take them overseas.

Pawnee Bill had been the Indian Manager for the Wild West, but at the last minute he decided he would not go to Europe with the Company, but would stay in America and organize a Wild West Show of his own. Cody and Salsbury considered the personnel of the Company, and decided to give Joe Hart the job of handling the Indians; so he was chosen to deal with the United States Government in making arrangements to take the Indians out of the country.

Hart experienced no difficulty in getting the graduates of Carolile, the Indian School in Pennsylvania, to join the Company, and he soon found that Black Cloud, a Chippewa Chief (then twenty-eight years old), would be a good leader of the Chippewa Indians with the Show. He chose Chief Flying Eagle, Chief Red Moon, and Chief Rain in the Face, as leaders of the different Tribes represented. In all, there were over one hundred real American Indians to look after. Joe seemed to understand the Indians, and got along with them very well, although he did have some problems.

An Indian belief was that if they ever crossed the ocean, they would waste away and die. It took a lot of talking to convince them that the white man did not waste away and die when he crossed the ocean, and neither would they. First, the Carolile Indians were able to see that they could do what the white man could. Kate, who was a graduate of the School, and a leader, helped to convince the more ignorant young Indians that she was not afraid to go, and gradually one by one they consented. Another difficulty with the Indians was the fact they could not stand to be confined in Madison Square Garden. It was damp, and they contracted colds and were ill.

Some of the horses and other animals had colds too; and all but one of the buffaloes died with pneumonia. That was a great loss to the Company, because they had to be replaced. Many of the performers also were ill, and needless to say, the entire Company was glad when it was time to sail for England.

Major John Burk, ever looking for anything that would be an advertising aid, had collected letters from some Army officers to prove to the English people that Buffalo Bill had been a genuine Scout, and a real soldier, and not a fake. The Governor of Nebraska had commissioned Buffalo Bill his aid-de-camp, with the rank of Colonel. The National Guards also gave him the title, which he used the rest of his life. The people of Nebraska claimed Buffalo Bill, the same as the people of Connecticut always claimed P. T. Barnum.

When the Wild West closed in the Garden, and while preparations were being completed for their sailing on the steamer, *State of Nebraska*, Annie and Frank went to Pine Brook, New Jersey, to shoot a match. It was a four-corner match, fifty dollars a corner, two shots on a side. The money had been deposited and a large crowd paid to see the Shoot. Annie and her partner won the match, the score being 94 to 91 in her favor.

Another match was shot in Philadelphia against one of the best shots in the world. They drew the largest crowd that had ever yet witnessed a shooting match. Annie lost by one bird, the score being 48-47. But Annie was pleased with her two matches, because she had some extra money to give her mother who needed help at that time, Grand Pap Shaw being now blind and ill.

The night after the last Shoot, Annie and Frank took the train and went to Ohio for a hurried visit with her family before leaving for Europe to be gone at least a year. They found her mother and Grand Pap Shaw as comfortable as they could be, made so by money Annie and Frank had been able to send them. But when they had to leave, it was with a sad heart Annie told them good-by, because she knew that ere she returned another loved-one would have entered the Heavenly gates. Grand Pap was a patient sufferer, and Hulda and Emily were doing all they could to lighten their mother's burden.

On this trip there was no time for the hunting or shooting they had always done before when they visited the home State.

In Scotland.

14
FIRST TRIP TO ENGLAND

THEY HURRIED BACK to New York just in time to take the steamer for
England. Annie, along with three hundred other people, was ready
to do her part to help make the first real American Wild West a
true success. There were roughriders from the West, over a hundred American Indians, some Mexicans, two hundred fifty horses—
many of them wild, and there were buffaloes, deer, elk, moose and
antelope.

Great preparations had been made for the trip, and nothing
had been left undone to make it a real, outstanding American company. They were going as messengers of good will to all the world,
and to show to the European people, the American way of life as
the pioneers had known it.

The steamer, *State of Nebraska*, had been chartered for the
voyage, and on the first day of April, 1887, they set sail for England, with London their destination. The voyage was not unevent-
ful, for they encountered a terrific storm which smashed the pro-
peller of the boat, causing the ship to drift helplessly on the sea
for forty-eight hours. For ten hours Annie was allowed to stay on
the Captain's deck, wrapped in a seafaring oilskin. Just why she
was allowed there, she never knew. The boat was dashed from side
to side, and she felt that at any minute it would capsize. As long as
the storm raged, the old Scotch Captain never left the deck. After
they had drifted two hundred forty miles out of the regular course,
the boat made a dangerous turn back toward London, and after
this real adventure, they finally arrived at their destination.

Nate Salsbury had perfect confidence that the English people would be interested in the Wild West of the United States, as the Company was to reproduce life as America knew it. They planned to take two weeks to rehearse, and to erect some buildings, for they hoped to stay in the one place six months.

The buildings had not been erected, nor was the arena nearly completed when the good-humored Prince of Wales (later Edward VII) came to see one of the rehearsals. The Management were distracted to think the Prince came to see the Show before they were ready. But the fact was, he was delighted with the manoeuvers of a hundred Western ponies that had never before been saddled, and. had never been shot over. And the cowboys were in their glory, too, for they enjoyed seeing how the new ponies acted in the arena for the first time. When a hundred American Indians came tearing in on their Indian ponies, the Prince decided the Show was strictly American, and returned to inform his Royal Mother that it was well worth seeing.

Soon the Queen sent a command that the show be given for her and her guests. A temporary Throne had been erected when she arrived with military escort, princesses, and many ladies-in-waiting. Before the performance, the American flag was borne around the arena by a horseman while Frank Richmond, the official announcer, called in his clear, loud voice, "An emblem of peace and friendship to all the world." As the flag was borne past the Royal Box, Queen Victoria and the English officers saluted the American flag, and that was the first time in history that English Royalty had saluted the flag of the New World.

After the grand entry, they staged a prairie fire and a stampede. Then they enacted the landing of the Pilgrims, and Pocahontas saving John Smith's life. Col. Cody, known to the English audience as "Buffalo Bill," with the help of a hundred American Indians and as many cowboys, staged the Massacre of Custer. The Pony Express rode in, changed his mount, and dashed off again, showing the way mail was rushed over the Western country. They also staged an attack on the old Deadwood Stagecoach, so named because of its service between Deadwood and Cheyenne. The battle between the Indians and the Scouts, and the rescue by Buffalo Bill and his Scouts, were very realistic. Cowboys roped and rode bucking bronchos, lassoed the wild buffalo, roped and branded wild steer. Buck Taylor lassoed and threw a wild steer by its horns, and single-handed tied it ready to brand. Jim Laurence did a rope act which only an American cowboy could do. And the Mexicans did their part, riding on their queer saddles with the high pommels from which hung their lariats. They handled their horses most skillfully, and one Mexican cowboy rode a horse in a race with a fleet-footed Indian by the name of Black Cloud, a Chippewa.

In the fall of 1939 I met Chief Black Cloud at a celebration in Birmingham, Michigan, when a new State road was opened that at one time had been an Indian trail. When my young son told the Chief that he had some Indian relics in his home which had belonged to Sitting Bull, Black Cloud asked him how he happened to have them, and when my son told the Chief that the relics had been given to his great aunt, Annie Oakley, the old warrior straightened up and told of his travels with Buffalo Bill's Wild West Show, and of their having been in England. He especially mentioned the first command performance they gave before the Queen and her guests and he said he never thought he could run as fast as he did that day. He told of Chief White Moon's marriage to an English girl, and of the death of one of the young Indians while there, which threw all the Wild West Indians into a panic, because of their belief that they would waste away and die if they ever crossed the ocean.

The handsome young Indian had died of tuberculosis, and they all thought they would die too. However, the manager of the Indians was able to convince them they were no more apt to have the disease in England than if they were in America. Black Cloud told me many interesting things about his experiences with the Show, more interesting to me, perhaps, because I, as a child, remembered him. At the time I met him in Birmingham, he was about ninety years old.

To go on with the program of the Show given as a commend performance for the Queen; the old Prairie Schooner drawn by its twenty ox-team slowly moved into the arena, showing how the settlers went into the Western country, a great contrast to the whirling, exciting act which had preceded. As the driver of the Prairie Schooner whipped up the lazy oxen with the long rawhide whip to hurry them along as they approached the exit, in rode Annie Oakley, alone a picture as she rode around the arena on her perfectly groomed horse that seemed to have a style all his own. She ended her race around the arena by riding up in front of the Queen's Box, and her spirited horse made a low bow to the audience. Annie's long brown hair flying in the breeze as she turned to ride to the center of the arena, was typical of the Western cowgirl.

Then in rode Frank Butler. He carried a basket of glass halls, and a gun for Annie. As they rode around the arena at breakneck speed, he threw the glass balls into the air, and she shot, breaking the balls, sometimes two, and even more, at a time. Then Annie stood upon the horse's back, and finished breaking the halls by shooting them as Frank threw them while he rode along by her side. They then dismounted, and the horses left the arena alone, for they knew that outside, back of the arena, was either an apple, lump of sugar, or a bright yellow carrot waiting for them.

From one side of the arena two cowboys entered carrying a kitchen table on which were placed a number of guns. They also carried in two trunks in which were mounted clay pigeon traps. Now came the remainder of the act: Frank stood about fifty feet from Annie and held a small, two by five inch card. Printed at one end was a small picture of Annie, at the other end was a small red heart an inch and a half high. With a twenty-two rifle Annie shot through the small red heart as many as fifty times in succession. Next Frank held the cards with the edge toward her and she using a pistol, would cut the cards in two. Sometimes they used a common playing-card, usually the five of hearts, and she would shoot through the card many times. Because of this trick, in later years all complimentary tickets to the theatre and baseball games were called "Annie Oakleys." She broke clay-pigeons thrown from the traps, not only one at a time, but as many as four. Frank would swing a cord around his body, at the end of which was a glass ball;

Annie would lie backwards over a chair, and with her gun upside down, would break the ball. Another clever stunt she performed, was to hold a pistol backward over her shoulder, and using a silver knife for a mirror, would break a ball that Frank whirled around his body which was tied on the end of the string.

When the arena grounds were level enough, Annie would ride around on a bicycle without holding to the handlebars, and shoot objects thrown into the air. She said by this time she was in good practice, and would prove it by shooting the ashes from a cigarette which Frank held in his mouth. Next he held a dime between his first and second fingers, with the edge toward her, and with a twenty-two rifle she hit it, sending it whizzing through the air. For days the boys around the Camp were busy trying to find the dimes.

At the end of the act, Annie ran and jumped over the table, threw three glass balls into the air, picked up a gun, and broke them before they fell to the ground. She threw the hot guns on the table, and ran as fast as she could to the back of the arena, and just before she went under the ropes that separated the arena from the side-seat section, she always stopped and gave a funny little dance and a kick, which made everyone laugh. All through her act no one ever knew what she was going to do next, she was so quick.

When the Show was over, the entire company lined up in the arena for the grand finale, and dashed out like a flash. At the very last, Buffalo Bill rode to the front on his beautiful white horse, and made a polite bow to the audience, and then dashed out as quickly as he had entered.

Col. William F. Cody, Buffalo Bill, about 1886.

15
ANNIE MEETS THE QUEEN

AT THIS COMMAND performance, the Queen had enjoyed the show very much, and as soon as the program was over she sent for Annie to come to her Box, much to the embarrassment of the shy little American girl. After greetings were exchanged, Annie said to the Queen, "My, what beautiful opera glasses you have." The Queen replied, "Why, my dear little girl, you may have them." And she handed them to Annie with pleasure. The glasses were gold and mother-of-pearl—a valuable treasure, and prized by Annie as long as she lived. However, she gave them to the writer a few years before her death, because she wanted to be sure they were in the hands of someone who would appreciate them.

After the Royal visit, the Management knew their Royal guests had been pleased with the show, and knew too, that the attendance of every person in London was assured. The day after the command performance for the Queen and her guests, the Wild West Show opened to what was considered the elite of all England, and at every performance for six months from twenty to forty thousand people were packed into the seats.

The morning after the opening of the Show, the newspapers' criticisms were short and to the point. One paper said it was a relief when Annie Oakley appeared, for they had seen so many people in the arena they were almost overwhelmed. Some of the critics said they had expected to see something, and they were not disappointed. The vast audience had been very appreciative, and never

99

had the Show gone better than at that first performance. The papers spoke of Annie's breaking the flying missiles with precision and dramatic effect, and all of the London papers were more than liberal in their praise of her work.

So many flowers were sent to Annie's tent, she could not care for all of them. They came from all over England, and some days there would not have been room for her to stand in her tent if she had tried to keep them all. She sent most of them to the women's and children's hospital wards in the Jubilee Memorial Hospital. It gave the little American performer a great deal of pleasure to share the choice flowers with people who had never had a flower in their sick-room, and not many days went by while she was in London that she did not send flowers at least twice a day by messenger. She received many "thank you" notes, and most of them said, "God bless you, dear lady."

Flowers were not all she received—gifts of all kinds found their way to her. One gift was a photograph in a hand-painted frame, of Princess Alexandria and the Prince of Wales, which was sent her by the Princess. Annie also received some pieces of valuable jewelry, one a diamond bracelet, another a valuable amethyst stick-pin to use as a flower pin. One of the most interesting gifts I think she had, was a pin of solid gold in the form of a bat, with the body of the bat made of moonstone, and the figure was so perfect even the eyes and the veins stood out which made it look as natural as could be. Annie prized the gifts that were showered upon her more than anyone ever knew, for she had never had so many things given to her before. However, she always wished other people could have so much too. People in need of the necessities of life were always on her mind, and she wanted to help them all. She never cared very much about wearing the jewelry she had, and never bought anything in the way of jewelry for herself.

It was a gay year in London—it being the Queen's Jubilee Year, all Royalty flocked there, and the homes of the best people in England were opened to Annie and Frank, as well as to other members of the Wild West company. There were many receptions and teas given in their honor, and Annie and Frank were welcome guests at the two Gun Clubs in London, a courtesy that had never before been extended to any other woman.

Annie shot her first live-bird match in England at one of the Clubs. She found that if she were to be rated as a first-class shot, she had to enter live-bird contests. Pigeon shooting at that time was one of the national sports, much as our golf tournaments are today. The class of birds used in England made shooting far more difficult and harder than any found in America. The birds were small and very fast, most of them were raised purposely for live-bird matches, and cost five dollars a dozen.

Annie was the first woman to shoot on the grounds of the London Gun Club, and she was presented by the Prince of Wales. For her first match Annie used an American gun trimmed with gold, which had a figure of herself set in the guard. The gun was a three-inch drop, and not a bad target-gun for that early date, but not good for those fast birds that made for the high wall like a streak of lightning.

At the first Shoot Annie attended at the London Gun Club, she shot very badly, and after the match an elderly newspaper man tried to cheer her up with the compliment, "I am delighted to have the extreme pleasure of shaking your hand. I expected to find a better shot, but not so much of a lady."

The fact Annie was such a lady was somewhat of a surprise to the English people, for they had expected to see a large, rather rough-mannered person. Instead, she was small of stature, very dainty and ladylike. She dressed in knee-length skirts, with leggings to match, that were laced or buttoned down the side. Her blouse waist was loose, enabling her to handle herself freely as she did the difficult performance. When the weather was not too hot, she wore a costume made of fine broadcloth resembling buckskin, (she never wore buckskin) but of course much lighter in weight. In hot weather, she wore costumes made of wash material, usually in shades of blue or brown. She always wore a large Stetson felt hat that turned up a little on the left side, with a gold or silver star near the edge of the brim of the hat.

Home in Nutley, New Jersey.

16

HAS FIRST GUNS MADE TO ORDER

WHEN ANNIE SHOT her first match at the London Gun Club she owned three sixteen-gauge hammer guns; they were good guns for that time, but did not fit her small shoulder, and made shooting more difficult for her than guns with the proper drop would have. However, a gunsmith was present on this occasion, and he fitted her with a gun made to her measurements, and presented it to her as a gift. Annie had never had anything that so pleased her, for at once she realized the perfect fit of the gun. On her next attempt to set a record at the same Club, she broke one hundred clay pigeons straight, making a perfect score. She then entered a match with the Prince of Wales, trying twenty-five of the fast birds, and made a score of twenty-three, winning the one hundred twenty pound prize. After that she shot many matches with the best shots in England, winning her share of the trophies at every match.

At that time there seemed to be a widespread interest in shooting skill, for at one of the exhibitions at the Club there were present the ruling Monarchs of five European countries, and the Queens of four. At that particular exhibition, the Prince of Wales presented Annie with a gold medal having a view of the London Gun Club embossed upon it. She had won highest honors in the match, and in presenting the medal, the Prince said, "I know of no one so worthy of it." Those words were also inscribed on the medal. The Prince also said, "America should be proud of you," and Annie replied, "I am proud of America."

Annie was willing to give her new gun due credit for helping her attain the perfect score, which in turn won for her the gold medal she prized the rest of her life. Having won such high honors at the London Gun Club, the gunmaker who had presented Annie with the gun, now gave her three more, all made to her measurements—one twelve-gauge, and two handsome twenty-bore guns. She treasured these guns highly and handled them with the best of care. Both Annie and Frank prized the four guns the London manufacturer had made, almost more than any other gifts they ever received at home or abroad. To them a gun which was fitted perfectly, meant more than just a gun. Frank seemed to be able to use the two twenty-bore guns with almost as much ease as Annie did; and in later years the twelve-gauge was my favorite gun, because I could make a better score with it than any other gun I ever tried, and I used all of her guns from time to time.

Perhaps the Gunsmith's kindness to Annie was repaid many times, for it was a clever piece of advertising for him to be able to say he had made the famous Annie Oakley's favorite guns. He owned a tract of land fitted up with every shooting facility. The land was only two and one-half miles from the Wild West Show ground, and he gave Annie and Frank the privilege of using his ground at their pleasure. Following the afternoon performance they often rode horseback to the shooting ground for a little match between themselves, sometimes taking some friends to join them in a pigeon match.

Five ladies wished to take shooting lessons, and formed a class. Annie consented to teach them, and charged them five guineas for each lesson. She used the money to provide some poor people with a few comforts they had never had before. Annie had previously reserved the right to give private exhibitions, and teach some if she wished, providing there was no publicity and no entrance fee charged.

She often entertained at affairs given on large estates, and the day following these exhibitions she always found a check for fifty pounds in her mail. A certain portion of this money always went to charity, and another went back to the small country place in Ohio to her widowed mother, younger sister and only brother.

It was after Annie won such high honors at the London Gun Club that the Queen sent her second command for a performance to be given for the Royal guests who had come for the Queen's Jubilee. Nate Salsbury conceived the idea of loading the greater portion of the Show on a train and sending it to Windsor Castle. This idea pleased the Queen very much.

The day of the performance the whole company were determined to do their best, and the Show went off as well as it ever had. Among the guests at this performance were Princess Alexandria; Prince Edward; Prince of Wales; the Princess of Wales; the Duke of Yorfl; King George of England; Princesses Victoria, Louise and Maude; Grand Duke Michael of Russia; the Kings of Denmark, Belgium, and Greece, and Saxony; Crown Princes of Germany, Austria and Sweden. More Royalty attended the show that day than had ever before been together at any one time.

In his comments on the roughriders, one London editor said: "Their ponies will buck for hours, only stopping for a fresh start. A pitching broncho, when at work on full time, is the most moving thing I ever saw. His spine seems to be made of whalebone, and he seems to possess all of the elements of a steamboat explosion, a high pressure piledriver, and an earthquake."

There were certain days every week while the Show, was in London when Annie held a reception for hundreds of people who wanted to know her and visit with her. Some people thought she must have trick guns to be able to shoot as she did, so she always had her guns unloaded on display, as were the medals she had won at home and abroad. Annie was always a gracious hostess, and no matter how tired she might be at the end of a performance, she would answer the hundreds of questions asked her by the guests who were anxious to know when she learned to shoot, if she shot in the field as well as being an expert in the arena, and many other questions. Two maids helped her serve tea, and there were two Bobbies stationed at either side of her tent who kept the people moving. Otherwise, they would never have gotten the people away in time for the evening performance.

Early one morning the following message was received in camp:

Col. William F. Cody.

Dear Sir:
Will the little girl that shoots so cleverly in your
Show, shoot a match with the Grand Duke Michael
of Russia?

(Signed) Edward.

Annie sent a message back that she would be glad to shoot a
match with the Grand Duke Michael of Russia.

They shot a fifty-target match, and the score was thirty-six to
forty-seven in Annie's favor. The Duke was supposed to be a very
good shot. Later Annie shot several other matches with him.

Annie's charming personality and wonderful skill had won for
her the admiration of all England. Frank had also enjoyed the attention she received, for he was very proud of her, and at the same
time much in love with her. People who knew Frank said that his
attitude was one of the secrets of her wonderful success—he was
able to allow her to receive the attention of the public, and not try
to claim even a little share of it for himself. He held the championship as the best shot in some of the States, and as a fancy shot was
almost Annie's equal. He originated many of her most difficult
shots, but when the unselfish husband and manager of the star of
the Buffalo Bill Show saw she could hold an audience of thousands
spellbound with her skill, he was ever more willing than ever to
step aside and put her forward. The more applause Annie received,
the happier Frank seemed to be, and the harder he worked to make
a success of her act. Just as Nate Salsbury made Buffalo Bill famous, so Frank Butler, with the aid of the newspapers, and, most
of all, the generous public, made the name "Annie Oakley" famous
around the world.

When the Queen's Jubilee was over, the Queen was tired and
went to Scotland for a rest, but as she was leaving London she
stopped at the Wild West grounds and sought an audience with
Annie. She asked Annie for her photograph, and later it was hung
in Marlborough House. Some of the questions the Queen asked
Annie were where was she born, and at what age she had learned

to shoot. Then she said, "You are a very clever little girl." To be called "clever" by the Queen, meant that she had received the highest compliment possible. The Queen also said, "I want to claim your friendship as long as I live;" and that she did, for they exchanged letters the many years that Queen Victoria lived after that.

Annie was reminded of the dream she had when a mere child, the night she was on her way home from the farm where she had been so unhappy, when she dreamed she had made friends with a real Queen and was so very happy. Thus, when Queen Victoria became so interested in her, Annie could not but feel that her dream of childhood had come true.

During the time the Wild West Show was in London, Buffalo Bill was jealous of Annie because of the attention she received from the public, as well as the headlines in the newspapers. He wanted her to receive enough admiration to be a drawing-card with his Show, but when it came to her having more headlines than he, he could not accept it without trying to prevent reporters and newspaper people from seeing her. There really was no reason for his being so jealous, because he as well as other members of the Company had a good share of the admiration. The Indians with the Show were treated like Royalty by some of the English people. Of course some of the Indians were educated, and enjoyed the attention they received from anyone. In fact, one or two English girls were quite in love with some of the young Indians.

Annie and Frank had so many invitations to spend the Hunting Season on estates of friends, they were obliged to decline many of them. However, they did accept a two-weeks' invitation from one of the oldest families in Shrewsbury. I remember the name very well, having often heard my Aunt and Uncle tell of the happy time they spent with Edward Clark, Esquire, his wife, and son, William. Mr. and Mrs. Clark had called on Annie and Frank so many times, they promised the English family if they had time to hunt any place, they would accept their invitation. And they spent two of the happiest weeks of their lives roaming over the great country estate, through the beautiful fields, and wooded hills, shooting partridge, pheasant, and black cock. Annie and Frank needed the rest and change after the busy six months they had just spent in London. They were invited to stay the entire Hunting Season, and regretted that they had promised to go to Germany to shoot for the Royal Family which prevented their doing so. Many times Frank told of the happy time they enjoyed with the Clark family, and many years later wrote an interesting story about it for a sports' magazine, which I have kept and will include it near the conclusion of this story.

17
ANNIE RECEIVES MANY LOVE LETTERS

ANNIE RECEIVED LETTERS from people in all walks of life, some were from hero-worshippers, others from "cranks;" many were real love letters with an offer of marriage, and some asked her for everything from a lock of her hair to her shoestrings. Just why Annie saved the letter I am quoting here, I never knew:

Earl's Court, London

Dear Miss Annie:

Can you ever overlook and forgive the intrusion that a broken heart is forcing upon you? I attended the opening of the Wild West Show in London, and after I witnessed your wonderful skill I bought a season ticket. I rarely missed a performance of your daily exhibitions, as days and weeks lapsed into months. It was not altogether your skill that attracted me, but your personality, your grace, your gentle bearing, and your sweet face with your expressive eyes that look out from under that broad-brimmed hat so becomingly worn. Your photograph (that I bought at one of the performances I first attended) has had a place of honor in my study ever since the day I bought it. I shall always keep it, although I do not need it as a constant reminder of one little girl in all the world that I ever did or ever can love. How I had hoped that some day we might meet, for until this afternoon I had never dreamed that another had come into your life.

Forgive me, I pray, for somehow I feel you will understand my stupidity when I tell you that I lost my father when I was a very small boy, and my mother, who is of gentle birth, brought me up very close to her. So you see my worldly experiences have been limited. I have explained everything to my mother. Should I stay in London I fear I could not trust myself to keep entirely away from your presence, though I shall never become known to you. I am leaving on the morning boat for South Africa. Forgive me for taking up so much of your valuable time.

Suffice it is this epistle, the outpouring of a broken heart, will be touched by your gentle hand on the morrow while I put distance between us.

(Signed . . .)

A few days later a young lady came to call on Annie, and she asked if she might bring a friend the following day. With Annie's consent they came; they were the mother and sister of the young man who had written the almost pathetic letter. Someone had informed them that Annie's manager was also her husband. The sister told Annie her brother was only twenty-one, and that his experience had been limited.

The mother, a tall, slightly built, faultlessly dressed woman, with a sweet face and expressive eyes, said she knew her boy could not love anyone who was not of the highest type. Annie told her she had not seen her son, so she was not to blame for his going to Africa to lose himself in the wilds, and the mother replied that he would be braver and even truer because of that strange love. The mother and sister left, and Annie never saw them again. But years later, after the young Englishman had spent almost his entire life in the wilds of Africa hunting wild game to make a collection of wild-animal horns, he came to America and met Annie and Frank.

Another love letter to which Annie made reference in her diary, was from a Count who watched her act every day for a month. After her performance was finished, while she ran to the rear of the arena, he would leave the grandstand and hide among the Indian tepees just across from Annie's tent. From that point he could watch and study the characteristics of the girl he dreamed of some day taking to France to his beloved mother. Among other things he said, He would kneel down upon a satin pillow and proudly introduce his wife, the Countess, while he placed a tiara upon her head which had been in the family for two generations. He also said that he had more of this world's goods than they could jointly spend, and that he knew from observation that she would be sincere, and that a sum of money would be placed in her bank account that would make her independent for life. The names of influential people were given as references as to his family and character. All of this was followed by an apology for daring to address her without a proper introduction, but if she would consider this proposal, would she write just one word, "Yes." And if her answer were yes, he would find a way for a proper introduction; but if she remained silent, he would feel the whole world had been lost to him.

It was unfortunate for him he had not taken the time to inquire into Annie's family affairs; he had evidently taken Annie's husband to be her manager. Soon after Annie received this letter, Frank wrote the Count telling him of their marriage.

I have often heard my Uncle say to Aunt Annie, if he were a little provoked with her, which was not often, "I wish I had let the Frenchman have you," and she usually answered, "I wish you had too."

Neither Annie nor Frank had time to answer the majority of letters she received, but Frank was always most courteous and did answer a great many of them. With his keen sense of Irish humor, he could see the amusing side of some of the letters, as well as the pathetic side of others. He would sometimes jokingly say, "If those cranks knew you as well as I do, they wouldn't think you are so nice."

It just wasn't done in those days, or the Prince of Wales might have been tempted to give up the throne for Annie when it came time for him to be crowned King. According to the custom of the time, he would not dare propose to an American girl. Then too, he had great admiration for Frank Butler, and knew that Annie and Frank were much in love, so the true friendship the Prince had for them both went on and on.

18
ACCEPTS INVITATION TO GERMANY

MEMBERS OF THE ROYAL FAMILY of Germany had been in London to see the Wild West Show, and then they invited both Annie and Frank to spend some time shooting with them in Germany. Crown Prince Fritz asked them to give an exhibition at the Charlottenburg Race Track. However, when it came time for the exhibition, the Prince was dangerously ill in Potsdam. The Emperor also was ill, being barely able to appear for ten minutes a day at the large window facing the court where the people waited that they might wave to him.

Because of the illness of both the Emperor and the Crown Prince, Prince William was detailed to do the honors. Annie and Frank both said then, that he was war-mad, and afterward he proved it to our sorrow.

The great audience which assembled to see the little country-girl who had been born in a log cabin, was more than appreciative. There were Princesses, Dukes, and other potentates lined up to see the exhibition, and they were held spellbound with Annie's accuracy and skill. After the exhibition Annie and Frank were driven to the Palace to meet the Emperor. He apologized for his absence from Charlottenburg. To him their visit to Germany was a message of good will, and he asked them how the Wild West Show might be induced to come to Germany.

When the Wild West Show left London, it went to Manchester, England, for several months before returning to the States. Annie and Frank did not go with them, because of Cody's attitude. But

113

the people of Manchester missed Annie in the arena, and were not slow to ask for her. Cody had not been too nice to Annie and Frank during the six-months' stay in London. He was jealous of all the attention she received from the people of London, as well as many people from other countries. While the Show was in Manchester, England, Cody brought his diary up to date, and in it he referred to Annie as the "lady shot." I was sure he regretted his attitude toward her all the rest of his life. He proved it in later years by doing all the nice things he could for both Annie and Frank.

Before the Show went to Manchester, Annie had been invited to go to France to shoot, but she and Frank needed rest, and so they returned to New York. They ate their Christmas dinner in the homeland. However, it was through their influence that the Wild West went to Germany within a short time for one of its most successful seasons.

After a month's rest in New York, Annie was busy making shooting records for herself, because with the four new guns that had been given her, she felt sure she could do better shooting than she had ever done before in this country.

The first to challenge her was the Champion of England, who had come over to see if he could not win the Championship of the United States. Annie had been challenged by him before she went abroad, but unavoidable circumstances had prevented their shooting the last two matches of the series.

The first match was scheduled for January, the seventeenth, at a Race Track near Philadelphia. Annie and Frank went the day before and stayed in Philadelphia all night. At two o'clock in the afternoon, the match was called. It was sleeting, and the temperature was down to zero. It was impossible to stop the clay pigeons within the open boundary. The Englishman grassed eighteen, and Annie fourteen, of the first twenty-five. She pulled up some in the last twenty-five, but the odds were too great, and the score was twenty-three in the Englishman's favor. Eight of Annie's birds dropped over the boundary line, being carried out by the gale; and he lost five in the same manner. Thus Annie went down in defeat. Her little twenty-gauge, with two and one-half drams of powder and three ounces of shot, did its best, but was out-distanced by the gale. However, the gate receipts covered the loss on the match.

The second match was arranged for January twenty-first, 1888, at Eaton, Pennsylvania. There the snow was covered with sleet, and the sun shone brightly. When Annie looked from her window, the snow-shovels were at work, forcing their way to the shooting ground. A path wide enough for two persons to walk abreast was cut through the drifts. The Gun Club used dark-blue clay pigeons on days like that, but shooting in zero weather was not shooting in comfort. The birds were first-class, and the score kept rather even until the last when the Englishman lost five birds straight, and Annie only one. Thus she had defeated the English Champion! As I have before related, Annie won the very first match in the series before she went abroad.

Frank E. Butler, as he was when teaching the children to shoot.

19
SHOW RETURNS TO AMERICA

IT WAS DURING the summer of 1888 that the Wild West sailed into the New York harbor, the cowboy band playing "Yankee Doodle" with all the vim and vigor they possessed. The entire company displayed the most brilliant colors they could find, and Col. Cody, a picture of American manhood, stood upon the Captain's bridge.

The Indians, all painted in their very brightest colors, and with their bright-colored blankets floating in the breeze, leaned as far over the ship's rail as they could to catch the first glimpse of the homeland. Many of the Indians had been seasick, and that, coupled with the other misfortunes they had experienced in England, which I have mentioned, made the Indians resolve, that if they ever got back to their own country, they would never leave it again. Cody, telling about the Indians' trip said, "They have been as sick as a cow with a hollow horn."

The newspapers in New York in glowing headlines told of the arrival of the ship, *Parisian Monarch*, saying that the flags of all Nations were fluttering in the breeze from every mast of the great ship, and that the harbor had never witnessed a more picturesque scene.

The Buffalo Bill Show had been a messenger of good will to all England, and had been accepted as such by people of other countries who had seen the Show. France and Germany both extended invitations for the Show to spend a year or so in their countries, which they did at a later date.

As soon as the Show was unloaded, it was set up on Staten Island where the public, by the heavy gate receipts, showed their approval of the trip abroad. But Annie was not there! The public missed her, and asked for her a great deal.

Major Burke, the clever advertising man for the Buffalo Bill Show, looked over the show business upon his return to Staten Island, and found that Pawnee Bill had started a pretty good show of his own during their absence. The Major used every means available to out-do the smaller company. One of the things he did, was to paste Buffalo Bill advertising over that of Pawnee Bill's, which read: "Wait for the Big Show: Buffalo Bill is coming."

The competitive fight between the two companies lasted for years. Pawnee Bill was a good Indian man, and at one time had managed the Indians for the Buffalo Bill Show; but for some unknown reason, Major Burke had always been jealous of him.

Annie had been busy making shooting records, and had won ever so many shooting matches. She and Frank were offered and accepted a contract with a new Wild West company.

The people in the new company were fine people and the salary was good for those days. After having been with the Buffalo Bill show so long Annie and Frank thought all Wild West shows were alike, however they were greatly mistaken. For when they went to the rehearsals they were much disappointed. The car load of horses from Texas and forty Comanche Indians had arrived and were the real things, but when it came to the cowboys, they were anything but real, some of them could not saddle a horse and do it right.

Frank wanted to do something about getting some real cowboys, but the show had been billed to open at a certain time and this did not allow them to send west for some good cowboys.

All the time Frank tried to form some plan, but nothing seemed to offer a solution to the problem. One day he was up early and on his way to Philadelphia, with his mind fully made up to tell the manager that under the present conditions he would have to cancel the contract. There were only six days to prepare for the opening to be held in the Gentlemen's driving park on the Exposition Grounds. The Buffalo Bill show was booked for the same place four weeks later, and Frank did not want Annie's and his name to be billed with an outfit that had not been a success.

Just as Frank reached the ferry he heard a newsboy yell "Paper sir." Frank bought a paper and having to wait twenty minutes before the boat came, he settled to glance over the morning paper. On the front page he read the headlines: "BUSTED AND STRANDED IN PITTSBURGH." The entire outfit of the Pawnee Bill show. Frank knew what had happened, for he knew Pawnee Bill was a good showman and knew what it took to run a show and how to make a success, he also knew there was not enough money back of the show to face bad business because of rain and cold weather.

As soon as Major Burke heard of Pawnee Bill's misfortune, quick as a flash sent the report to the newspapers, and well Frank knew his game. Frank had always liked Major Burke and Pawnee Bill as well, but had felt rather sorry that the feeling of jealousy existed between them so now wished that he might do something to help Pawnee Bill.

Frank looked up from his paper and saw the manager of the little new company. He rushed to him, showed him the paper and told him, "There isn't a minute to waste if you see things as I do. Accept my proposition. It will not cost much over two thousand dollars to free Pawnee Bill, and bring his outfit to Philadelphia. You will have real cowboys in your show and good equipment, more good Indians and some buffaloes."

They wired Pawnee Bill, and the manager rushed to Pittsburgh. Frank helped him put up the money, and almost immediately after he arrived, Frank had a wire from him, "Landing the outfit on a special. Meet me at the park ten o'clock tomorrow."

When the manager saw the Pawnee Bill's cowboys, he knew he had made a mistake in accepting the company of poor riders. He paid his would be cowboys two weeks salary and sent them on their way. The real rehearsal started. Everyone did his best in the short time that was left. On the day of the opening they had everything shined up and looking new. It was a fine day and in parade, the saddle trimmings and spurs on the horses looked like new diamonds.

Everyone was in parade, including Annie and the little dog that had been hanging around just for fun. Annie tried to look her best for she thought she owed it to the dear old Quaker city.

The streets were jammed with people to see the parade and it seemed that everyone was in an extra good humor.

Even Major Burke was on the street to see what kind of a parade the new company could put on. He was dressed in his spotless linen as was his custom, with a white silk handkerchief for a tie. He stepped from the sidewalk to speak to Annie saying, "Frank is responsible for all this." Nate Salsbury and Major Burke both saw the show that day, and afterward came to Annie and Frank and told them that they had never seen better work by their own company. They praised the manager of the new company, for he was new in the show business. The fact was, that being willing to listen to Frank put the new manager as well as Pawnee Bill, on his feet.

Salsbury said, "Annie, you don't belong in this show. It is all a mistake. The people expect to see you back in your place with us." Her reply was, "I realize all that, but here I am free to shoot as I like, and I do not have to see the press kept away from me for fear they may give someone except Buffalo Bill a headline." When she and Frank said "Goodbye" to Salsbury and Major Burke that night, they felt a little sad, for truly they were friends, and they had always been friends and fair.

After doing a good business during the stay in the Park the show went on to the big ballpark in Glouster, New Jersey. This was an unknown place and advertising was necessary, so an Indian wedding was advertised. The Indian couple were married according to Indian rites. Eight thousand persons witnessed the ceremony.

All the rest of the season the show did a good business and when Annie and Frank left the company at the end of the season there were regrets on both sides, because they had enjoyed helping the little company. And Pawnee Bill had been most grateful to Frank for helping him save his company, and the manager of the little company never could thank him enough for the help he gave him in bringing Pawnee Bill and his outfit on from Pittsburgh to join his company. It was a happy arrangement all the way around, and a partnership that lasted a long time.

20
ANNIE MAKES NEW SHOOTING RECORD

ANNIE AND FRANK went to New York after they had left the little company in New Jersey. They had a busy winter, and always told of the good time they enjoyed. Annie and a friend, by the name of Jim Pilkington, shot a one hundred picket match with a pair of shooters, by the name of Ditmer and Jacques. They shot at West Farms, New York. Annie and Pilkington won the match and carried home the prize money. This match attracted a lot of people for there were many interested in both sides thinking their side could win.

Among many of the newspaper notices they got after the match was, "Annie Oakley, in her wonderful fetes of marksmanship, scored the greatest hit of the event."

Another one read, "Annie Oakley, the rifle queen, was the wonder of the spectators."

Special to the *New York World*: December, 1888—"Annie Oakley broke fifty birds straight, beating all records." In a match one shot at fifty birds, for fifty dollars.

One match which caused a lot of comment was the one in which Annie beat Miles Johnson, the champion of New Jersey. One newspaper in Philadelphia ran the headlines, "Annie Oakley defeats Miles Johnson, the champion of New Jersey in a match of fifty live pigeons, Hurlington Rules." Three thousand people saw or tried to see this match, the traps had to be moved three times, as the vast overflow from the grandstand closed in. To have beaten Johnson seemed to have been an unusual thing, because as long

as I can remember, all shooters have told about this day as being a
great one in the history of the shooting world.

The *Baltimore American* in its comment on the shooting wrote,
"Beaten by a Girl!" Annie Oakley outshoots Miles Johnson, conditions fifty birds each. Score, Johnson, forty-two; Oakley, fifty.

Another good shot of note was John Lovet. The newspaper notice of their match read, "Annie Oakley defeats Lovet. She knows
how to handle a rifle, and this week has been receiving admiration
and applause for her wonderful skill. She has just defeated Lovet
who is somewhat of a shot himself and has a reputation, in this
neck of the woods, that good shots envy. Annie appeared in a short
skirt, otherwise jauntily dressed. Twenty-five birds each was lib-
erated at thirty-one yards, she threw her gun against her shoulder
instantly, upon the liberation of each bird, and brought down one
after the other, she scored twenty-five and her opponent scored
twenty-one."

The *Dayton Herald* wrote, "Annie Oakley is a brilliant little
star in the sporting world. The reason why she does not proclaim
herself champion shot of the world, we do not know. But for all
that, for pure and simple practical shooting, no other woman lives
that can equal her."

In March of 1889 Annie and Frank had a conference with Nate
Salsbury who asked them to return to the show with him, and to
go to France that same year. They planned to travel through seven
other countries. Every inducement was offered to get them to go
abroad, for Salsbury knew the public would expect to see them.
The fact was that they wanted to continue some study abroad and
renew old friendships. Cody promised Annie he would look over
the horses on his ranch and give her the best horse he could find.
They agreed to go, and at once began to make plans for the trip.

They never had a written contract with the company; neither
did Buffalo Bill ever have a signed contract with anyone else.
Everyone knew that when Buffalo Bill said a thing he meant it and
his word was good.

One of the first things Annie and Frank did was to go out to
Ohio to visit her family, for they knew their second trip abroad

would keep them away for several years. This time they found that there had been an addition to the family; two nephews and a niece had come to join them. Her mother was quite comfortable all alone in her little home, for by this time all the family had been married, and had homes of their own. Annie and Frank loved children, and had a delightful time getting acquainted with the new little members of the family.

For all the rest of their lives they could tell us what we looked like and what we did, even though we were then only little bits of humanity. I happened to be her niece and namesake, and the only niece that came into one of her own sister's family. I have often wondered if this was the reason that in later years she wanted me with her most of the time. They spent much time with my mother and father, or with her mother in the little old log house, for it had been all remodeled with money Annie had sent home. Always when she won a shooting match and the prize was a money prize she felt a few extra dollars could go to help make her mother a little more comfortable.

The old neighbors had not forgotten her, and when she came home they always came, dressed in their best to see her, for they liked to hear about her trips and the shooting matches. She usually brought her guns with her and would do fancy shooting for them. The more sedate country men thought she had lowered her principles to travel with a show, but after they knew Frank they changed their minds.

Missie tells of experiences with the show.

21
A SECOND TRIP TO EUROPE

APRIL, 1889, FOUND the Buffalo Bill show ready to set sail for
Europe to be there for the great Exposition Universal in Paris. The
day the show was loaded on the big ship was not like the day they
sailed into the harbor upon their return from England. The rain
came down in torrents, and everything that went on board was
soaked. The woe begone looking Indians were drenched to the skin,
and as the buffalos were hoisted aboard their great shaggy manes
dripped like wet cedar trees. The voyage was not as rough as the
previous had been, and they landed sometime in May.

The show was loaded on a train at LeHarve and was taken to
Paris. There they began to make ready for the grand opening.

Annie was delighted with the little horse Buffalo Bill had sent
on to her from his ranch, for she had tried him out on the training
ground. They opened to a French audience of twenty thousand
people. Through the first part of the performance, the people chat-
ted indifferently among themselves. Salsbury looked blue as he said
to Frank and Annie, "Be ready to do your act, any minute." Salsbury
could somehow read the pulse of a great audience in any country,
and he felt that this first performance would either make or break
their success in France.

At this time Frank did not work in the arena with Annie. She
had two well-trained, fine looking cowboys, and Frank helped the
management look after some important details. The act was called,
Annie had been announced. She rode into the arena between two
perfect riders. The audience ceased their chatting, but no friendly

welcome greeted her as had been the case elsewhere, but she felt the "You've got to show me" air greeted her. Her determination seemed to answer back, "I can show you and I will." Even the horses seemed to sense the attitude of the people, and stepped around the arena with a little better style than usual. The band played with more spirit than ever before, for Billy Sweeney was proud of his cowboy band and could do his best upon such an occasion.

Frank noticed two groups of three or four men, standing at either corner of the reserved seats. They had started to applaud some of the other acts. It was the custom in some countries to hire what they called clackers who would start the applause for each artist, and for this favor the artist would tip the head clacker enough money to share up with the rest. Annie wanted honest applause or none, so the management got the clackers out of the way.

At the first crack of the gun, she sent the target into a million pieces, the first sound from the audience was "Ah." Then the shots went so fast that the cry of "Bravo" went up.

The little new horse was a wonder and seemed to sense the situation and was, in himself, a real picture as he carried his new mistress around the arena as fast as he dare to go. As the act was finished and Annie tossed the last hot gun upon the table, she bowed to the roaring audience, that by now was battering hats, throwing handkerchiefs, and yelling themselves hoarse. The next act was kept waiting while the cheers brought her back time after time, at last she ran to her tent, and while the audience kept up their cheering, she quickly changed to a riding habit, and mounted her little horse.

As she mounted he was anxious to get into the arena, and if ever a horse went at full speed he did. The audience voted Annie a most wonderful shot and a real horsewoman, and the French people were just as generous in their praise as the English had been.

The twenty thousand people stood ready to fight for Annie and her little horse, Billy, during their six months stay in Paris.

The newspapers were, also, very liberal in their criticism.

One of the papers in the comment said of the opening, "When the whirling exciting affair was over, Annie Oakley held a regular court where everyone paid homage to her. Journalists of all nations, statesmen of all nations, but she was thoroughly at home, for she received everyone with a graciousness that won all hearts." Another paper dated May 19, 1889, "Annie Oakley came in with hearty cheers as she smashed one after another of the flying objects. Later when surrounded by a court of admirers, she was asked what she thought of her reception, and the French audience. Her reply was 'I am delighted with my reception, but I am so hungry I must have my dinner.'" Annie was much admired by the French press men for her simple bearing.

Three days after the opening in Paris, an invitation came for her to shoot at the Circle des Patineure. The next day they sent a carriage and repeated the invitation, which she accepted. The courtesies of the club were placed at her disposal, during her stay in Paris, and she was elected an honorary member, a distinction of which she was proud. She and Frank often spent a pleasant morning at the club, or perhaps an hour in the afternoon after the performance was over. At the club they met many charming people, among them were M. Sadrnot, the president of France. He paid her the highest compliment by saying, "Annie, when you feel like changing your nationality and profession, there is a commission awaiting you in France, with the army."

Diana Salifour, King of Senegal, after seeing the show in Paris on July 12, 1889, offered Buffalo Bill one thousand francs for her, and when Buffalo Bill said, "Why, the lady is not for sale," he asked what he wanted her for. The king told him that in his small villages his people were not safe for the man-eating tigers carried many of them away. The King thought that with Annie's wonderful skill the danger would soon be past, but he begged of Cody to release her. When Annie told the King she did not wish to go, he went down upon his knees, and with the sweeping grace of that of the knights of old England, he lifted her hand, raised her fingers to his lips, then departed with the air of a soldier.

Old Parisians told Buffalo Bill that they never before had seen such a splendid representation of all Paris society at any show.

Buffalo Bill gave breakfasts at which Dukes and Counts and Barons were present. He loved to have great feasts for his friends and always provided the best that was to be had in the land. To his friends when he was away from the show he was called Colonel Cody.

Artists were always present in the Wild West camp making studies of Indian life and of animals. They were particularly interested in the Percheron draft horses, which they had never seen before. It was then that Rosa Bonheur made the portrait of Colonel Cody. French fashions called for cowboy hats upon the streets of Paris. Indian blankets as well as bows and arrows and moccasins, and bead work were sold in the souvenir stores.

After a six month stay in Paris, the show closed with regrets, for the entire company had been treated as royal guests. Not to be out done by the English people, the French held out the hand of great hospitality to the Wild West people.

In November the Wild West show went to Marseilles, where they were received with the same appreciative sort of audience as they had been in Paris. While they were in Marseilles, Annie and Frank were entertained at eleven o'clock breakfast at the shooting club by the president of France. They shot at the rifle range in the morning, and at the live bird traps in the afternoon. A high stone wall encircled the boundary, which was twenty-five meters from the traps. Annie was justly proud of her shooting that day, for she either won or divided every sweep she shot in. Ninety-six of the best blue rockets fell to her gun. After this using a double barrel thirty-two twenty rifle, she shot at two rocks at twenty-five meter mark. She grassed them both. The club had them mounted and placed in the club house as a memento of her visit to Marseilles.

The day's shooting swelled her bank account, but the meeting of loyal friends meant more to both Frank and Annie than the money. She was presented with a beautiful gold medallion somewhat larger than a hundred dollar gold piece. The club had it made for her. She so appreciated the gold medallion that, for the rest of her life, she wore it more often than any other piece of jewelry she had.

After the show left Marseilles it went to Lyons, where they kept a fine pigeon club called, "Society des Sports." They too, gave a fashionable breakfast in Annie's honor. There she shot well, but someone else shot better. She always told about leaving this club with her hands in her pocket to fill them instead of the usual cash she usually won, for in France the prize for the highest score was cash.

That day she had been presented with a gold medal as a token of the affection that the people there had for her.

After the show closed in Lyons the troupe needed rest, and the equipment repairs if they remained there for some time.

Annie and Frank made a tour of Southern France where they participated in several matches. Annie's membership in the Circle Des Pitineau at Paris entitled her to compete in any match in France.

The kind of powder used in the shells had a lot to do with the winning or losing of all matches. By the time Annie shot the match in Lyons, the Schultz powder she had brought from America was all gone, and she had to use French powder. Her lack of confidence in the load had something to do with her losing the match in Lyons.

It was not until Annie began to shoot in France that her real trouble with gunpowder began. The first time she tried the French powder it was smokeless. Frank loaded the shells according to the directions upon the can, but he found out later that they had used a wet weather load on a very hot day, so the barrel of one of her guns burst. However, no one was injured. After the accident they had with the gun, they had the shells loaded every day and did not trust the weather man to make the report. They found that many of the shooters in France used English powder, and that many of them had brought a supply over on private yachts or had it smuggled into the country in some way. At that time the government would not allow powder made in another country to be brought into France, even though the powder made there was of inferior quality for target shooting.

Annie and Frank went back to Marseilles to shoot a second match. The day after they arrived they received notice that there was a package at the custom's house for them. They had received a letter from England with no signature. The letter said that two dozen fresh eggs had been sent to them, and not to throw away the package until Annie had tried some of the contents in her gun. At the custom office they found a large tin box securely wrapped. They could not understand at first why it took such a large box to hold two dozen eggs. When they opened the box, they found the eggs had been packed in Schultz powder. It had been sent to her by some good English friend that knew the supply she had taken with her would soon be gone. The duty on the box was forty cents, which they gladly paid.

The good Schultz powder gave Annie such confidence in the load that during the three day tournament in Marseilles she in her life never shot better. Annie always gave the unknown English friend the credit for helping her to win the match. Never in her life was she more surprised at her good shooting for the shooting at Marseilles at that time counted on her record toward winning the championship of France.

The last match Annie shot in France was at Lyon, where she won a beautiful medal of oxidized silver and two hundred dollars. As the golf ball and club are important in the winning of a golf game so the gun and powder are important in the winning of a shooting match.

While the show was in France, Annie had a little French maid of whom she was very fond, and the maid called Annie Missie. Frank soon adopted the name and in later years Annie's family and her best friends always called her Missie.

22
NOT MUCH SUCCESS IN SPAIN

FROM FRANCE the Buffalo Bill Wild West went to Spain; Barcelona was the first city played. It was a sad day for the whole company when they arrived there, for the city was stricken with the Spanish influenza.

The Wild West people had the flu, smallpox, and typhoid fever all at the same time, and lost Frank Richmond, the official announcer, and eighteen Indians. The loss of Richmond meant a great loss to the show, for outside of being well liked and a real gentleman, he was a great help in giving the impression that the show people were a fine type of folks which they really were at that time. Buffalo Bill and Nate Salsbury were always particular to have the very best people in every department and in later years many of the show people became leading business people in the States.

The fact that they did not lose more people with the dreaded diseases was that the Wild West show carried its own fine physician. Frank managed to keep well and was a great comfort to Frank Richmond to the last. The day Richmond died Annie was taken ill, but was able to put up a good fight for her life.

Frank arranged services for Richmond, and the Indians carried on their usual service for the Indians that had died one after another. It was a sad time for the whole company for in the far away land they were as one big family, and felt the loss keenly. Frank could never talk of the death of his good friend Frank Richmond without saying that was one of the very saddest days of his life.

131

The show went from Barcelona to Madrid, where the stay was almost fruitless. The Wild West people did not like the Spanish bull fighting, and the Spanish people almost mobbed Buffalo Bill when he said that his cowboys could rope and ride the bulls.

Naturally they played to empty seats, so the stay in Madrid was not enjoyed by any of the Wild West company.

Annie found that the Spanish people were not very good marksmen. The main reason was that they were more interested in the national sport of bull fighting. The only powder in Spain was black powder and a very inferior grade, and they had no smokeless, but Frank had powder sent in from England as it was not against the law of Spain, if a heavy duty was paid.

The Spanish people were very kind to Annie and Frank and they liked them, but they felt sorry for the many beggars, and never did forget the sad people they saw there.

When the smallpox and typhoid became so bad, and the Wild West was in danger of being quarantined, they sailed on a wretched old steamer for Naples. At first the pilot refused to take the steamer outside of the harbor. It seemed providence was with them, for there had been a big storm just ahead of them, and one came just after they had crossed and entered the bay. Either storm would have meant almost certain disaster, but anything seemed better than to stay in Spain and face the awful epidemic. Just when the company doctor would get people on their feet, someone else would have been exposed, and trouble would start up again. Everyone was glad to go anywhere out of Spain.

After three days and nights in the little old boat on the Mediterranean, they arrived just at day break. The sight of the beautiful bay, with Mount Vesuvius looming up in the background was one never to be forgotten. The bay was filled with the Italian navy, and the warships gave the salute to the American company as they steamed into the bay.

While the Wild West was in Italy they hoped to recover some of the losses they had had in Spain, due to the frightful diseases.

The show went well, and the Italian people were very appreciative and liked the Wild West people, needless to say the show people could see they were going to enjoy Italy, which they did.

Annie and Frank went to the crater of Mount Vesuvius, while the Indians staged a war dance in the shadow of the mountain because they were afraid of everything. One day Annie was standing where she could see the mouth of the crater, and someone heard her say, "Oh, the wonder of it all." This gave the friend an idea; he bought Annie two paintings, one of the volcano in action, and one of it when it was quiet. These Annie added to her collection of gifts to bring back to America with her.

While in Italy Annie had a peep into the narrow streets of Naples where the scum of the country seemed to live. She was told that some of the people were deformed purposely by their parents in order to make them good beggars. Cripples were looked on with envy, for they were sure to make more money than those less deformed.

There were many good shooters in Naples, and several fine trap shooting clubs. Annie and Frank enjoyed the people there and spent a great deal of time in the beautiful homes.

In Italy there was no smokeless powder, but loaded shells could be sent into the country by paying duty on them, but no powder came in bulk. Annie had her shells loaded with powder and sent in that way. Then they unloaded and reloaded them properly to insure a perfect load.

They visited Pompeii and Herculaneum. While they were at Pompeii they found many objects of interest. One was the ruins of a house that had been the home of a sportsman. The walls were covered with beautiful paintings of a game scene of some kind. One picture a marsh scene seemed to be set into the wall of what might have been a fireplace. Out of the rushes in the foreground, a number of birds that looked like English snipe were rising; in the back was a sportsman in the act of aiming at the birds with a queer looking gun at his shoulder. In the museum at Pompeii, they also found several old pistols which had been taken from the ruins. They were encased in lava, and would have crumbled away if the lava had been removed.

March, 1890, found the show in Florence, after a very enjoyable time there. They were loath to say goodbye to friends they had met there. But they moved on to Bologne, and there was little of interest there, and no shooting club. Annie was glad the stay in Bologne was short. The next place the show went to was Milan, a beautiful clean city, and the home of many good shooters. Their bird dogs were something like our pointer dogs except that they had longer ears, and here they found one of the finest shooting grounds in the world.

The shooting ground was situated in the center of an old stone arena that dated back to 1425, and had a seating capacity of around thirty thousand. The enclosure was two hundred yards long and one hundred yards wide. A running stream encircled the arena; therefore it was necessary to cross a bridge to get to the arena. The live pigeon traps were set between the seats and the grass plot. A low wire fence marked the boundary which was about twenty-five meters, the birds were good, being brought directly from the mountains.

There were true sportsmen in Milan, and Frank liked to tell about one in particular who was an Italian gentleman. He had gone to South Africa to hunt lions. When he was notified that his manager had robbed him and had disappeared, and that he should return at once, his reply was, "I am on the track of a lion, and cannot leave."

Annie, in telling of their stay in Milan, spoke of there being few beggars there, and that every man from the nobleman down to the most humble driver seemed to be a gentleman. At the gun club Annie and Frank received the most courteous treatment, and she won some very fine prizes. Thus far the Wild West had enjoyed every moment of the time spent in Italy.

Statesmen as well as the elite of Rome attended the Wild West performance. In all the experiences of the show people they had never seen such enthusiasm and appreciation as in Italy, and most of all in Rome. Every performer can do his best when an audience is appreciative, so it was, with the Wild West. Even the animals learn to love applause.

The twentieth day of February, 1890, the entire Wild West company went to the Vatican to attend the coronation of Pope Leo XIII.

Every member of the company was dressed in his best, and the Indians wore a little extra paint as they always did when they wished to dress up for a special occasion.

The Wild West people lined up along the corridor through which the Pope was borne to the throne. The Pope spread out his hands in token of blessing as he passed Buffalo Bill. Had it not been for Major Burke who himself was a Catholic, the Indians would have let out a whoop of approval as he passed them, for Major Burke had spent some time training them for the occasion.

Annie's description of the service was that it was a grand sight to see the Pope's fine face as he distributed his blessing to the right and to the left upon the thousands of people who had gathered there. The Pope was carried around on a throne by eight men who passed between rows of soldiers. He had a standing army of three hundred soldiers who guarded him.

While in Rome Annie and Frank spent as much time as they could studying the fine old paintings. They said what a privilege it was to go back over the years of struggle, and realize that something far greater than mere human brain lay behind the spiritual minds of those great artists.

One day they went with a guide to see an old castle that was being dismantled. Here they saw a caretaker piling up a lot of rubbish to burn. On the pile were two paintings. The men were going to kick them out of the frames, when Frank said, "Oh, give them to us," which they gladly did and they were packed with the rest of the treasures to be taken back to America.

Annie was showered with gifts of every description, and every courtesy had been shown her that could have been bestowed upon a queen. It was with much regret that after a month's stay in Rome, the company moved on to Florence.

In Florence there was a large American colony that greeted the American company. They extended their hospitality to the Wild West People by giving them a big feast, the Indians and cowboys were included. Some of the students had to confess they had to go to Italy to see an American cowboy and an Indian. The Italians thought it quite a joke that few of them had ever seen Buffalo Bill.

The people of the Wild West who enjoyed art loved Florence as they did all of Italy. The stay in the interesting country ended in Verona. Here they gave the performance in an old stone arena. On the day of the opening when the ticket box opened at one thirty there was not a person in sight, all agreed that the company would leave Verona on Milan receipts. But lo, the people of sleepy old Verona had only been taking their afternoon nap, for in less than an hour, about sixty thousand people began to pour into the seats, and kept coming until every seat was filled. Such appreciation was never shown before unless it had been in Rome.

Buffalo Bill thought the best fun of all was when he had been in Venice. He and some Indians had their picture taken in a gondola gliding on the Grand Canal. The Gondolier, an unique personality, attempted in his own way to tell them about everything they were seeing, regardless of whether they could understand him or not.

The Indians had staged a war dance near Mt. Vesuvius and their bright colored blankets with the gay headdress made an unusual picture with the volcano looming up in the background.

All of the Wild West people had liked Italy almost more than any other place they had ever been because the Italian people were so appreciative and seemed to enjoy the show more than any thing they had ever seen. The attendance had been greater than the heads of the company had ever dreamed of. It was with regret they left a country where everyone had turned out to show their appreciation.

The Wild West went to Bavaria, and at the first place they showed, a lot of American students greeted them at day break. The management of the show was so pleased that the students were asked to have breakfast with the show people. It had been such a surprise to hear the loud cheers of the American colony as the special train rolled into the city that Cody ordered a bountiful breakfast for them. In a short time all was in order, and the usual performance was staged.

The next morning a messenger arrived from the Regent, inquiring for Fraulein Oakley. After a low bow he stood at attention while he delivered the message. "If convenient, his Majesty requests the honor of an audience with Fraulein Oakley at ten thirty this morning." The request was granted and the Regent arrived. There was no display. He came unaccompanied and unadorned, except that his coachman and his footman wore the royal ensignia.

Annie and Frank felt that they were greeting an old friend. His voice was low and kind, and after a long chat they went into the arena. He had said that he would like to have a coin that she had marked thrown into the air and hit with a pistol bullet. Annie marked a coin or two and he had just put them into his pocket, when a bucking horse came right at the Regent. A cowboy had led the horse up and had mounted it some distance away, the cowboy had been helpless when the horse had gotten the bit between his teeth. He did not know a royal personage was near. Annie had warned the Regent of the danger of the horse coming at them, but he had replied, "I don't think he will hurt us." However, she saw the danger in time to leap to his side, she held onto his arm and they both fell to their knees as she pushed him over. The infuriated beast struck the regent's right shoulder, but did not hurt him much. He took it all good-naturedly, and smiled while the dust was being brushed from his otherwise spotless attire. After a pleasant eleven o'clock breakfast served in Annie's private tent, the Regent left giving Annie and Frank a cordial invitation for the near future.

The next day the Regent sent a handsome cigarette case to the rider of Dynamite, the horse that struck him. He also sent a valuable diamond brooch, with a crown and monogram to Annie.

Dynamite was the best bucking horse that Buffalo Bill had ever sent from his T. E. ranch. At some of the performances a cowboy would lead him to the front of the arena and the announcer would say that if anyone in the audience would care to ride the bucker the management would give him a sum of money. One of the cowboys would come out of the audience dressed like a town boy. He would shake and say he thought he could ride him. After much preparation, he would mount, and in a few second was off on the racing, pitching, prancing, throwing bucker. Not many times did the show ever have anyone from the audience willing to risk his life on Dynamite's back.

One day Annie and Frank were shown through the palace where the mad King of Bavaria was kept. They were told that the royal house had forbidden the King to marry a beautiful peasant girl and the King's reply was, "She will grace the throne, or I shall never be your King." The late Empress of Austria said, "that he was just as sane as we are." Annie and Frank were very sympathetic and full of understanding and liked the King. He became fond of them, and before they left Bavaria he gave her a valuable onyx bracelet that was inlayed with mosaic so fine that in order to see the real design, one has to look at it through a magnifying glass.

Before the Wild West left Bavaria, Annie gave an exhibition for the benefit of the poor. For her services the Baroness Rothchild and Openheimer gave her a handsome diamond brooch.

The show had been well attended and the company had enjoyed their stay in the small country.

Before going to Austria, the Wild West agent was informed that there was no smokeless powder in the country, nor would any be allowed to enter with or without duty. Having plenty on hand, Frank packed it in two shot bags, and hid it in a mattress and pillows. Some of the bags were packed in the box with the lamps, and many other places. When the company arrived in Austria and began to unpack, it seemed that every place they looked was a bag of gunpowder. As far as the shooting went the first exhibition was a failure, due to the fact that some of the powder that had been packed with the lamps had been oil soaked, and the shots sounded like squib fire crackers.

The Emperor of Austria asked that Annie and Frank be shown into his presence. He arose with a smile and greeted them with a real handshake. He was tired and somewhat troubled so asked them to go hunting with him, which they gladly did. His game preserve was seventeen miles out from his palace and horseback was the best method of travel. They got an early start, and hunted several hours when the Emperor had plank fish and other dainties that had been prepared and served in their honor. The deer hunting was good but Annie said she somehow could not shoot at a deer there, because they seemed so contented.

At Dresden the show had good grounds and people filled every seat, and here the Duchess of Holstein and her daughter, Princess Fedora arrived. After greetings had been exchanged, and Annie had been presented with a handsome bouquet by the princess, Annie had breakfast served for them. Annie and Frank were asked to hunt on the King's game preserve. There they were told that they were allowed to shoot one buck each.

One fine morning three bucks came out into the open field of buckwheat to eat their breakfast. The guide whispered to Annie and Frank to shoot but neither could shoot one that time. They said it was a shame to shoot and spoil their fun, so they gave one loud shrill whistle and in a second three pairs of heels disappeared into the forest.

After a few months travel through other countries the Wild West people were glad to be back in Germany, Maybury, and Bronschweih, and Liepzig, then on to Berlin, and to renew friendships that they had made while they were there before.

During the winter of 1891 the show went into winter quarters and Colonel Cody came back to America to do some hunting and to visit his family. About Christmas time there was a report that Annie had died in Germany, but it was soon contradicted. The following letter is one Frank received from Cody while he was in America.

Horth Platte, Neb.
Jan. 19th, 1891

Dear Frank and Annie:
I received your nice Christmas card, and would have acknowledged before, but I've been off to the war. Just got back today, I had a thousand soldiers out. Burke is so stuck on it, he won't come away. I think he is going to marry a squaw. Old John Nelson got scared out and ran away, and never stopped until he got to North Platte. Well, my dear little girl, I actually cried when I first heard of your death. Then I got to thinking it over and made up my mind it was

not so. I cabled Frank and received no answer, and I knew full well if our Annie was dead Frank would have cabled me. Will be glad to hear from you. When does your birthday come?

 Love to you both,

Colonel

It was at this time that Old Sitting Bull was killed, after President Harrison had stopped Buffalo Bill from trying to capture the Indian for fear he might be killed.

In a few days Cody wrote to Frank again.

At home
Jan. 27th

My dear Butler:
Yours of Jan. 13th received and found me at home. The Indian war quit but may break out any time. Burke left for Washington yesterday, got home without his bride, says he left her in New York. Now Frank go ahead with the ammunition. You know what we want so you order it.

 I can't say when I will be back, or whether or not I will come through London, but if I can I will cable you. I am so glad our Annie ain't dead, aren't you? Got your letter with a letter from V. C. and glad you sent them.

 Love to Annie and yourself,

Col.

23
BRING FOREIGN TROUPES TO AMERICA

MAJOR BURKE was the advertising manager for the Wild West. He had come to America with Cody, while Salsbury was in Germany as head of the company in winter quarters. Salsbury was busy thinking what he could do to improve the show. He had sent men to several countries to make arrangements with the different governments to have troupes join the show. He wanted to bring them to America, so he could put on a Congress of Rough Riders of the World at the World's Fair in Chicago, in 1893. Salsbury always looked ahead to have something different and his dream was to have a company that represented every country in the world, as messengers of peace and good will to all the world.

Joe Hart was the advance man for the show in Europe. He spoke several languages and was a diplomatic man. Salsbury thought he would be a good man to send to Russia to make arrangements with the Czar to have a troupe of Russian Cossacks join the show.

Before Hart went to Russia he had met Sir Thomas Lipton who asked Hart to go with him as his secretary, for he saw that he was a young man of ability. Hart would not go because he had promised Cody and Salsbury that he would stay with the Wild West while they were in Europe. Then too he had promised Salsbury he would go to Russia for him.

When Lipton found out Hart did not have a written contract with Cody he saw no reason why Hart could not go with him. Hart told him that no one with the show ever had a written contract. Lipton shook hands with Hart and said he wanted him for his friend so long as they both lived. They were both young men then, and the friendship did last until Lipton's death in 1933. (Uncle Joe, as I always called him, was visiting in my home at the time of Sir Thomas Lipton's death.)

Then Uncle Joe Hart told me more about the great friendship that had lasted over forty years. Lipton never missed sending Uncle Joe twenty pounds of his best tea for Christmas and for a great many years Aunt Annie, Uncle Frank and I enjoyed sharing the tea that Lipton was so generous to send. In fact we were drinking of the tea at the very time the message came that our good friend had died.

Uncle Joe had just had a letter from Lipton's secretary telling him of his expected visit to America, and of how he was planning to take him on his yacht for a cruise, for when Lipton came to America they always had a delightful visit on the yacht together. As they grew older the friendship seemed to grow closer for Uncle Joe was the last of the Buffalo Bill Company.

All during the Winter in Germany Annie was for ever doing all she could to cheer the homesick cowboys and Indians, and she saw to it that they wrote home as often as they should. If any member of the company was ill she was on hand to see that they had what was best for them to eat. The company doctor did his best to keep every one well for being away from home so long was bad enough for some of the company without being ill.

After the winter in Berlin, 1891, the show moved on to Russia with a certain degree of success, but by this time the Wild West people were homesick and tired of traveling so nothing was much of a thrill to them.

Annie did some shooting with the Grand Duke Michael, and won everything in the way of prizes that was offered. She was photographed shooting a deer in Russia, the picture was used later as a lithograph for the show's advertising.

One gift that Annie prized was a Russian Cossacks cape. The cape was made out of goat's hair hammered into shape and not woven. They were snow white and could not be seen by the enemy in the snow-covered country, and were large enough to cover the rider and came down over the horse's body so the snow and rain did not touch the horse, and the heat of the horse kept the rider warm. Very few of the capes ever left the country so the one Annie had is one of the few in this country today.

The Wild West people were so homesick that one day Frank heard a Russian swearing in English and he told some other members of the company and they all ran to see if it might not be an American. The fact that they did not like Russia made the entire company dissatisfied, so when the announcement came that the show would go to England for another six months they had a feast of rejoicing, for they knew they would be going back to America after that.

As far as gate receipts were concerned in Russia the company had been well satisfied but the country was not as interesting to most members of the company as other countries they had worked in.

The English people welcomed the Wild West company with open arms in much the same manner as they had when they arrived the first time, and they made the time spent there almost as thrilling. For six months they played to packed houses and Annie and Frank as well as other members of the company were entertained royally.

White Moone, one of the Indian chiefs, married an English girl and did not return to America.

One death that occurred was that of Lone Wolf an Indian who died of old age. No one knew how old he was. He had always said, "Heap plenty old." Uncle Joe had been fond of the old fellow and liked to tell us of his burial. Lone Wolf had carved on a cross a picture of a crouching wolf. This was placed upon his grave as a headstone.

When the company were ready to return to America they counted the horses they had to bring back with them and found many of the horses had died with the glanders in England.

All in all the four years they had spent in Europe were thrilling and profitable for most of the company.

No one felt quite so badly as the company physician over the losses through death, for they had been more than he had hoped they might.

At the Chicago World Fair.

24
THE CHICAGO EXPOSITION

Now came the preparation for the great exposition in Chicago. This meant trips to Washington to make arrangements with the government for more Indians to go from the reservations, to join the Buffalo Bill's Wild West Show. The advance agent made trips to Chicago, to rent the ground and arrange for the privilege of entering the city and staying for the period of the exposition. They could not rent space inside of the exposition grounds for the management of the World's Fair thought the show would not be dignified enough, so they rented fourteen acres just across the street from the entrance and the show opened a month ahead of the big fair.

P. T. Barnum, the showman, had suggested to the exposition management, they should place on exhibition the mummies of Pharaoh Rameses II and his family, as well as the mummies of the daughter of Pharaoh who saved Moses from the bulrushes. The men in charge of selecting the exhibits had turned down Barnum's suggestion as well as other subjects he had tried to interest them in. During the colorful career of the famous showman he never missed an opportunity to get personal publicity, nor acting antics for his show's advertisement.

In 1870 P. T. Barnum organized his first circus after having had thirty years experience in presenting freaks and pranks in the museum world. He had been called the Prince of Humbugs so to try to interest the Chicago World's Fair committee in his circus was not a new experience to him after having had in his circus such freaks as the Siamese Twins, General Tom Thumb and the two famous giants M. Bihin and Col. Goshen an Arab. One great attraction in the early days of the show was the family of Fiji Cannibals. The picture of Barnum's Woolly Horse being chased through the Rocky Mountains by brave soldiers is one that has been familiar to everyone acquainted with the circus posters even during the gay nineties.

The American public had been interested in Barnum's curiosities and performers as well as his menagerie and circus, so the pleasure loving public was ever looking for something new to be presented by the Buffalo Bill show, after they had made such a successful trip abroad. The fact that Barnum had died in April, 1891, perhaps helped to turn the public eye upon the Wild West that was to be presented in Chicago for a period of the most successful run it had ever had in America, up until that time.

While the arrangements were being completed for the opening of the Wild West for the 1893 season Annie and Frank rushed to Ohio to have a visit with her family. There was great rejoicing when they arrived, and we were all on our best behavior. It was interesting to hear them tell of the time they spent abroad. All of the family was greatly interested in all of the medals and gifts that were packed into the trunks. As usual the neighbors were invited in to help enjoy the famous couple's interesting experiences. Frank was as full of jokes and fun as ever, so for the smaller members of the family he wrote the Croaker.

THE CROAKER

Once on the edge of a pleasant pool.
Under the back it was dark and cool,
Where bushes over the water hung,
Just where the creek flowed over the bog,
There lived a grumpy and mean old frog,
Who'd sit all day in the mud and soak,
And just do nothing but croak and croak.

Till a blackbird hollered, "I say yer know,
What is the matter down there below?

Are you in trouble or pain or what,"
The frog said, "Mine is an orful lot;
Nothing but mud and dirt and slime,
Fer me ter look at all the time,
It's a dirty world." So the old fool spoke,
"Croakity, croakity, croakity, croak."

"But you're looking down," so the blackbird said;
"Look at the blossoms overhead.
Look at the bees and the butterflies;
Look up old feelee. Why bless my soul;
You're looking down in a mus'rat hole."
But still with a gurgle, sob and choak,
The blamed old critter would only croak.

And a wise old turtle who boarded near,
Sez to the blackbird, "Friend, see here;
Don't shed no tears over him, fer he
Is low down' cause he wants to be;
He's one o' them kind er chumps that's glad
Ter be miserable like and sad.
I'll tell you something that ain't no joke.
Don't waist your sorrow on folks that croak."

Aunt Annie, not to be outdone by Uncle Frank, could not write poetry for us small children, but she could make us laugh with her funny pranks. One day when she happened to be sitting on the grass with us in the shade of a tree in the edge of the woods she took a piece of paper and tore off little bits, wet them and pasted them on their eyelids, forehead, chin and ears and put larger pieces on her cheeks. Then she began to make funny noises and wiggle her face. We all just loved such pranks and never thought we could do them as well as she could do them.

I do not remember how long the visit lasted but it was soon over. April, 1893, found the Buffalo Bill show ready to open to packed houses, in fact the day the Fair opened thousands of people were turned away. People bought tickets for the Wild West show thinking they were going into the Fair. When they found out their mistake, they were all satisfied and thought they had had their moneys worth.

The day the show opened the rain came down in torrents, and the lot being a little low, became a regular mud hole. Annie Oakley in her diary wrote that the horses made their way through the mud as best they could. When Cody opened the show he introduced the new features. As he appeared in front of the big audience he made a fascinating picture mounted upon his snow white horse. He was proud to introduce one of the new features, The Congress of Rough Riders of the World. No longer could he say that the show was a production of the West. For in the grand entry rode the American Cavalry, British Lancers, French Chasseurs, German Eulans, Arabs, South American Gouchos, the Russian Cossacks, along with the Mexicans, Indians and American cowboys. There were four hundred performers in the arena; the entire company consisted of six hundred.

In the street parade and in the arena the Congress of Rough Riders carried flags of all nations, as messengers of good will to all the world. No one that saw the show could ever forget the daredevil riding of the Wild West Congress. I have heard people say that saw the opening of the show that the Congress of Rough Riders rode like fiends.

It was a wonder how the Arabs could ride as they did and not get their long flowing robes tangled up with their horses' feet. When they dismounted they did some acrobatic tumbling on the ground and then climbed into a pyramid that one Arabian giant supported. The Ulans of the Potsdam Reds wore shining breast plates and polished helmets, and displayed the German colors.

The French troops, twenty or more strong, wore bright blue coats and scarlet trousers. These were the French Chasseurs.

The British Hussers and Dragons wore different uniforms as they were different regiments.

There was a regiment of American soldiers that did maneuvers to the amusement of them all. The Russian Cossacks contributed to the puzzle with their trick riding. They had won for themselves the name Wonder Riders of the World. People differed as to which group were the best riders as they tore around the arena at break-neck speed.

The Indian exhibit was one not to be forgotten by anyone who saw it. Cody had moved the shack that had been Sitting Bull's to the show grounds, and some of his prized possessions were exhibited there also. Chief Standing Bear wore the most gorgeous head-dress one could imagine, it was made of over two hundred eagle feathers. Chief Red Cloud, Red Bear, Kicking Bear, and the ever interesting Chief Rain in the Face, lame as he was, all helped to make the exhibit a real success as did the hundred other Indians who were happy to be a part of the show.

Buffalo Bill, Johnny Baker, and Annie Oakley all did some of their best shooting during the fair. Annie had a wardrobe of thirty-five different costumes. They were all very much the same style but differed in material and color. All of the costumes portrayed the same neat appearance in every detail. Frank had tried out many new shooting stunts before he could decide which the public might be the most interested in. Annie was always willing to improve her act by adding interest to it. One of the new shots she added to her act was to throw six glass balls into the air at one time and hit them all before they struck the ground.

Annie and Frank made many new friends in Chicago, and she became better known to thousands of Americans than she had been before they went abroad.

During the Fair the show played to over six million people with no expense of travel. They had cleared in cash an even million dollars. Cody had made enough money that at the close of the Fair he went to North Platte, and paid off the debts of five churches, bought the band a new outfit, and did several other things for the town.

At the close of the show after the busy season of 1893 everyone felt the need of a rest, so Annie and Frank made a trip to their favorite spot in Ohio where they could enjoy a few quiet days before they went on to Nutley, New Jersey, where they had planned to build their first real home.

After the close of the World's Fair, Annie and Frank went to the farm in Darke county, Ohio, where I lived with my mother and father and my brother then about four years old. This was the first real recollection I have of seeing my aunt and uncle and a happy recollection it is. It was a happy day when the long clothesline was stretched out in the sun and the clothes and costumes were all hung out to air. There seemed to be so many clothes that I felt sure they were going to stay a long time for surely it would take a lot of time for the things to be brushed and pressed and packed away for the next season. I know now that some were to be discarded, some were to be mended, and there were new ones to be made. My resourceful mother helped my aunt to do this, for in those days there were no drycleaners. Old-fashioned tailors still did the cleaning and pressing that was done.

Aunt Annie always went over her clothes at the end of the season and made sure she had everything ready for the next season, for when they made long stands she liked to have many changes of costumes, sometimes as many as thirty-five different changes. After everything had been gone over by brushing, sponging, and pressing with the mending all done first they were packed in fresh tissue paper, so the garments would not wrinkle. After they had been worn for months many of the costumes would look like new because they had been cared for so well. Theatrical people often marveled at the condition of everything in the trunks because of the fresh appearance clothing had after having been packed away for months. Often Aunt Annie showed other people who traveled how she packed her trunks, and they were delighted to learn some of the secrets of packing.

I have not forgotten one day when mother was working on a dress for Aunt Annie—it was to copy a dress that she had seen in Paris and the pattern took all of the material they had with none to waste. I was busy sewing for my doll, but when mother went to put in one of the sleeves she found I had cut up the sleeve to make my doll a dress. Mother wanted to punish me, and my aunt picked me up and kissed me and said mother could have the old dress to make over for me. It was yellow silk, a sort of a crepe I think. She also said when I grew up I could make her a dress to pay for the material I had spoiled, which I did and many more. Aunt Annie was my staunch friend ever after.

We were interested in hearing Uncle Frank tell about the new peep show machines that Thomas Edison had made. Some of the first pictures he had made were of Buffalo Bill and Aunt Annie shooting.

They were making a lot of machines and selling them at a real profit. The demand seemed to be for the screen machines and Edison had told Uncle Frank that if they put out ten of these machines that would be sufficient to show the pictures to everyone in the United States. Edison himself was not in favor of making too many of the moving picture machines for he was afraid of killing the legitimate stage show as well as the out of doors show, such as the Wild West and the Circus. He was right for it was not many years until the moving picture did take the place of the out of door show, by taking its toll of the Wild West patrons. At that time Annie Oakley and Buffalo Bill were better known to everyone, both young and old, than anyone else in America or abroad.

When Aunt Annie and Uncle Frank were in my home it was so confusing to have two Annies in the same house. Since I had been named for my aunt, there was a constant misunderstanding as which Annie was wanted. When the show had been in France Aunt Annie had had a maid whose name was Annie, so she called Aunt Annie Missie. Cody liked the name and was the first to adopt it. When Uncle Frank thought of correcting the confusion he decided to call Annie Oakley Missie; it was not long before all the family liked the name and to her best friends and family she was always called Missie.

We thought if we had a nickname for our aunt it would not be out of place to have one for our good-natured uncle, but it was several years before we found one that seemed to suit him or that we thought we dare to call him by. One time when Missie was ill he came into her room and started to do funny stunts to make her laugh and she said to him, "Now Jimmie, the squirrel does tricks" and from that time on she called him Jimmie when she wanted to

be funny. The next time I went on a trip with Missie and Uncle
Frank I heard her call him Jimmie and after that I always called
him Jimmie and it was not long before the rest of the family
adopted the name. It did not take long for the closest friends to
fall in line and the last years the famous couple lived they were
known as Missie and Jimmie. It has always seemed more natural
for me to speak of them using their nicknames, so from here on in
the story I will refer to them as Missie and Jimmie.

I cannot remember when Missie and Jimmie were not a part of
my family, for when I was a child almost every year after the show
closed for the season they came to our farm to hunt and work on
the new stunts for the act for the next season. Part of the time they
kept a fine riding horse on the farm for practice. When my brother
and I were quite young we were taught to ride and shoot. We were
astonished the first time we saw Missie stand straight upon her
horse's back and shoot the glass balls thrown into the air. She could
lie down on the horses back, or hang from her saddle while doing
trick shooting.

As young as we were, we were interested in hearing Missie and
Jimmie tell about Salsbury trying to find something new each year,
so that the people could not say the show was always the same. I
can remember too the sympathy my mother and father felt when
they were told that Salsbury was forced to leave the company because of ill health. Missie and Jimmie had the feeling that something dreadful had happened. The level head of Salsbury had been
a definite reason for the show's success. The ever-thoughtful
Salsbury had gotten the best out of every member of the company
because he had proved to the people he had given them the best of
everything that could be obtained.

After Salsbury was forced to give up work the Wild West never
made as much money as before. Gate receipts dwindled. For one
thing the show was run on a different schedule; there were more
one day stands, instead of playing weeks and even months in one
place as they had done before.

After Salsbury's retirement soon after the World's Fair ended
in Chicago, James A. Bailey became part owner in Salsbury's place.

For twenty years or more Bailey had been part owner of the Barnum and Bailey show and he had a little different idea about the show business. After the Barnum and Bailey fire in winter quarters in November, 1887, when all of the animals had been destroyed except thirty elephants and one lion, Bailey had helped Barnum build a bigger and better circus than ever. He thought he could combine Wild West and the circus but it did not seem to go so well. It seemed clowns and cowboys did not go together. Bailey's idea of not feeding the company well and not taking quite such good care of the stock did not seem to please the public either. In the farm country the well cared for stock that Cody and Salsbury had to show seemed to be a great attraction to the stock man and the average farmer, and for the show to be in a good farming country in the late eighties and the early nineties always meant good business and large gate receipts.

It had been a custom of Bailey's to do things and then consult Barnum, which Barnum did not object to in his old days, but Buffalo Bill had always been taken into consideration when Salsbury wanted to do a thing. It was always hard for Cody to reconcile himself to Bailey's way of doing things and he never was happy and carefree after the Bailey interests came into the Wild West. Barnum had been happy with Bailey planning and doing things his own way so long as he was allowed to have the center of the stage as far as publicity went, and Bailey was smart enough to allow the famous showman to have the lead in publicity for he knew he was the best advertised man in the show business and it was Bailey himself that advertised the Greatest Show on Earth, which was the Barnum and Bailey show.

At the time of Salsbury's death Missie and Jimmie thought things with the show would never be the same and they began to plan to retire so they selected the town of Nutley, New Jersey, as the place they thought they wanted to build a permanent home. It had been a dream of theirs to sometime have a quiet home of their own.

My mother often talked about the plans they had made while they were with us during the winter of 1894, for it was in the new house they hoped to put all of the trophies and the things they had gotten from all over the world where they had worked and visited. Missie and Jimmie had worked and hunted in fourteen different countries.

After the comfortable house had been finished Missie found housekeeping a hard task, though she had always wished she could settle in a house and stay. However when the time came each year for the show to start out she was ready and willing to start. She had traveled so long that she felt more at home in her cozy little tent and sleeping on the train than she ever did in a house.

All during the busy years Missie had spent traveling she had never forgotten her mother's little home back in Ohio, for, from time to time, she had sent money for repairs, and for comforts she wanted her mother to have as she was growing older.

Soon after the house in Nutley had been finished someone got the idea of giving an amateur circus for the benefit of the poor. It was after the panic of 1893 that so many people had been out of work, and without welfare organizations such as we now have, money was needed badly to help out people who had been out of work. Everyone in the town that would was put to work to produce a real amateur show. Nutley being strictly a residential town many New York business men had their homes in the picturesque town, and they were willing to do what they could to make the show a success. They had wealthy men selling peanuts on the seats and they liked it. Years after when I first went to Nutley to visit, people who had lived there at the time of the circus laughed and told me of the fun they had doing the work of a candy butcher or perhaps riding a funny old horse that was well known around town as a delivery horse, and many other jobs that had been given them. The good that was done with the money earned at the amateur circus has never been forgotten by many of the town's people.

For the next three or four years Missie and Jimmie traveled with the Buffalo Bill's Wild West Show, and things went along pretty much the same for them, although through the Bailey interest the show was fast changing from the old original Wild West to a combination Wild West and circus. Circus people were added from time to time and a midway with regular sideshows was put in front of the Big Top gates. Cody and the old performers did not like the idea of fire eating freaks, slight of hand performers, and snake charmers being added to the once Wild West. Cody had taken a circus man as his partner, so what was he to do.

Missie and Jimmie were not so happy in the Wild West as they had been and began to look forward to the time when they could retire and live in the simple way they thought they would enjoy. After about two years they found that keeping house and traveling with the show did not mix very well, for they could not be at home long enough at any one time to pay to keep the house and to close the house made too much work to open it for a few weeks, when they could be at home.

They always seemed to be having the unexpected thing happen that caused a lot of trouble. I remember of hearing Jimmie tell about one time when they had been away, birds had built a nest in a chimney that was in the dining room. They built a fire in the fire place and could not stand the smoke and the only way they could think of to clean it out was to shoot up the chimney, so he did. With the birds nest down came all of the soot that had accumulated in the chimney, and it spread all over the light dining room carpet as well as to leave the soot marks over most of the house. Poor Jimmie was in bad with the housekeeper as well as Missie. When I first heard him tell the story I asked him what he ever did? He told me he had business over in New York for three days so he went without even saying good-bye to anyone. When he returned he threw his hat into the house first to see if he dare come in; when he found that the mess had been cleaned up and that Missie was glad to see him back again, he felt at home once more.

Missie found it hard to keep help in the house because she was too particular and exacting and made the hardest work of the simplest task. After having had a rather strenuous time trying to keep house and work for the Buffalo Bill's Wild West they rented the house and later sold it at a loss and never went back to the house they thought they were building for a permanent home.

As Nance Barry in The Western Girl.

25
HEARING THE STORY OF SITTING BULL

JIMMIE TOLD INTERESTING stories of the Indians and I was greatly surprised to learn that the Indians were not trained to do all of the things they did in the Wild West, but merely lived as they would have had they been on the reservation. Kate, one of the squaws that traveled for many years, had been a student at Carlisle, as well as some of the other Indians that seemed the most intelligent.

During the days of the Custer Massacre Chief Sitting Bull had been a bitter enemy of Buffalo Bill, but through Missie he became a good friend of the showman. When he went to Washington to see the president, he gave him the name of the "Great White Father." After seeing the people in the East the chief said, "That if every Indian killed a white man for every step they took, the dead would not be missed." He went back to the agency and told the tribes, that the Great White Father would give them justice and protect them. The time the forty or more Indians spent with the show was conducive of great good for the first time Sitting Bull went back to Standing Rock he told every Indian what they had to fight against.

After the fierce Sitting Bull was with the show Missie taught him to write and he gave her the first photograph he ever autographed. It was no wonder that one of the features of the Wild West in 1885 was the Sioux chief whose band had wiped out Custer's army in the bloody fight. The people who came to the show looked upon the fierce looking Chief with awe. He was stooped shouldered with extra long arms and crooked legs, a huge head and shiny eyes. When he was not bedecked with plenty of paint and his gorgeous band of eagle feathers he wore a plush coat, black flowered trousers and a bright orange and red tie. He liked a shirt that had flowers in it if he could find one, and wore as much dirty jewelry as he could comfortably carry, and a few fur tails here and there. He also wore a large crucifix, although he was not a Catholic. People who really knew Sitting Bull liked the old fellow for he was good hearted. His week's salary was always gone before the next pay day. Most of his money went back home to his two wives and eleven children. The rest he would give to youngsters who came around his tepee to see him, and he could not understand how so much wealth could go by unmindful to the poor.

The chief had learned much during his travels, but while he was off with the show some Indians made arrangements that a lot of land between the Missouri river and the Black Hills should be settled by the whites. When Sitting Bull got back to the agency he and some other Indians objected to the invasion. At the camp near Standing Rock Agency, the high priest of the Siouxs made their people go through the awful agony of war dances. Several hundred at a time would dance around in a circle, jumping in all directions shouting and moaning until they fell to the ground. Sitting Bull became one of the leading dancers. He danced until he was nothing but skin and bone. Lone Wolf in his translation of the Great Spirit had said that the earth was bad and worn out, and that if they would be constant in their dance, the Great Spirit would give them a new place to live. After the old time war chief decided that the war or ghost dance would not get them a new place to live, he decided to fight again.

The government agent thought Sitting Ball should be captured, so they set out to get him. It was during the winter of 1891 and Buffalo Bill had just returned from Europe leaving the show in winter quarters in Germany. Cody had started out in a long hunting trip when he heard that Sitting Bull needed to be captured, so he started again with a lot of cheap jewelry, candy, and gaudy trash of every description. President Harrison was afraid that Buffalo Bill would be killed, so stopped him from going on. It is said that if the president would have let Cody alone that he would have captured Sitting Bull with a sucker. Instead three or four weeks later on a cold December morning, the Indian police walked into Sitting Bulls camp to take him, he seemed to be willing to go with them. His son taunted him by saying, "You have been a brave man and now you give yourself up to the police." In a few minutes the Chief called several hundred of his ghost dancers, and started the fight. It was the last fight the old warrior ever saw, many of the dancers were killed including Sitting Bull himself. Not long after the Indian warfare ceased forever.

It was not for some time however that Missie and Jimmie knew of the death of Sitting Bull, for they were in Germany. He had written them shortly before his death. The letters were written just after Buffalo Bill had gotten back from wanting to capture the Chief.

It was not until the Wild West got back to the States and Missie and Jimmie were with us that they knew Sitting Bull had left a will leaving his prized possessions to her. They were his pipe of peace with the headdress and uniform including the moccasins which his daughter made for him to wear in the fight against Custer. Missie and Jimmie had two letters the same month from Buffalo Bill and just why they kept them rather than some others I do not know. Unless it was because of the false report of Missies death.

I had seen my aunt and uncle go through their act many times but had never seen the show. One can imagine the excitement the day my mother had a letter from her sister, my aunt, telling her that the show was to be in a town near enough that we could see it. When I saw the first lithographs of the Buffalo Bill show pasted upon sides of barns in the country, and on empty buildings and bill boards, it was as a wonder to me. On the lithographs they had my aunt's picture doing all sorts of shooting. They had her billed as the "Peerless Wing and Rifle Shot of the World." They also called her "The Champion Shot of the World." Although she never claimed the title.

The day we were to see the show for the first time seemed to me about the most important day I had ever experienced. We lived about twenty miles from Piqua where the big show was to be and we had to drive a horse, so we had to start very early in the morning, to be in Piqua in time for the afternoon show. We drove a good horse but it seemed to me we would never get to the show ground. We started so early that the dew was so heavy it dripped from the fringe on the carriage, and every minute I expected to hear my mother or father say it was raining and that we would have to turn around and go back. That was the very thing that had happened the week before when we had started to a Sunday school picnic. A friend of my father's by the name of Amos Kimmel, of Versailles, Ohio, and his wife had gone with us in a double carriage, and after I found out the grown-ups were as anxious to see the show as we were, I felt a little surer that we might continue our journey.

My mother had made me a pretty new dress and it was all starched as stiff as could be, she had made my brother a new waist with ruffles around the collar and cuffs and they were starched and ironed as slick as could be. The dampness from the early morning dew made our clothes wilt and all the way mother was worried because she had wanted us to look our best. She got the idea that if we got to Piqua in time we could go to her sister's home who lived there and she could heat an iron and press all of our clothes, which she did.

Perhaps you can remember the quick little jerk in your heart when you saw a circus tent for the first time. When we arrived at the show ground there were so many tents and wagons it looked to me as if we were lost and that we could never find Missie and Jimmie. Everyone with the company seemed to know that Annie Oakley was looking for her relatives and her family, so it seemed that everyone tried to tell us where to find them and in a few minutes we were in front of the private tent that stood under the big top at the end of the side seats.

We were all made comfortable and made to feel at home, and soon we were filled with wonder when we were taken to the big dining tent where we ate our dinner. We were very hungry after our long trip and everything was really good. The dining tent was equipped with plain board tables covered with red checked table clothes. We sat upon plank seats supported by tressels. The tables were made in the same manner and they took up little space when packed into the big wagons. After we ate we went to see the cook wagon. Three sides let down to form additional floor space. The upper half was raised to form additional ceiling, thus in warm weather it made an open air kitchen

We saw the cook handing out great dishes of good food to people who took it to long tables. We went to see the table where the bread was sliced, and wondered if there could be enough people in the world to eat so much bread. In response to our questions, mother told us it was no small task to prepare and serve meals to three hundred and fifty people and travel from one town to another almost every day, where different arrangements had to be made for food. We learned that what they called an "advance man" went thirty days ahead of the show and made arrangements with the town merchants to furnish food and supplies needed. Not only for the people but more than two hundred and fifty horses had to be fed beside a herd of buffalo and the cattle.

We visited the horse tents, and saw long lines of well-groomed horses. They looked so comfortable in their clean tents standing in plenty of fresh clean straw. The same thing was true of the oxen, and buffaloes. My father talked to the boss hostler, and when father said he liked the way they took care of their animals, the hostler took us to the blacksmith shop that was set up under another tent. In the shop all of the draft horses were kept shod. The saddle horses were not shod for they were not rode over paved or cobble stone streets. In the blacksmith shop all of the wagons and other equipment were kept in repair, and the shop traveled around as an integral part of the equipment. The boss hostler told us that the stock was all cared for under the direction of a skilled veterinarian. The animals seemed to be the pride of the show and people who were interested in animals marveled at the condition they were in, and at how contented they seemed to be.

When Jimmie took us into the big arena we wanted to know why there was no tent to cover the arena that looked like a big field. The seat sections formed a horseshoe shaped arena and the only part that was covered with canvas was the seats. Jimmie told us that if the arena was covered there would have to be tent poles

in the center of the arena like the big Barnum and Bailey Circus. That would never do in a Wild West for the cowboys and the bucking horses could never dodge the tent poles. Then too the top of the tent would be shot full of holes in a very short time.

There was a heavy canvas wall at the back of the arena, behind which was an enclosure for the purpose of protecting the performers in bad weather, and keeping the public out. At the back of the arena were the Indian tepees, where the Indians spent most of their free time during the show. This gave them a real camp and a place to call home. The Indians with the show were mostly Sioux's at that time. We experienced quite a thrill when we heard Jimmie talk to them in their own language.

The squaws did bead work to pass the time, and because they liked to do it. They had made Buffalo Bill a buckskin jacket beaded solid. There were two small papoose in the camp at that time, and we were greatly interested in them as they were the first Indian babies we had ever seen. All of the Indians took great pleasure in showing off when they were dressed up, and liked to have someone pay attention to them when they were not too tired.

Buffalo Bill's private tent was under the big top at the end of the side seats on the opposite side of the arena from Missie's tent. We stopped to visit with him and admire his trappings, and his fine horse that was tied to a tent pole near his tent. His guns too were on display in a rack at the entrance of his tent. We were much interested in his broad brimmed hat and his high-heeled boots.

When Buffalo Bill picked me up and stroked my long curls, and told me I looked like my aunt I was a happy little girl. He asked me if I had a gun and when I told him I did not have he said he would send us one as soon as he got one to take the place of a gun he was using, which he did that same summer. I told him I was sure I could shoot as good as my auntie if I had a gun.

After having seen around the camp we went back to Missie's tent where there was a big pitcher of lemonade waiting for us. We watched with delight as Jimmie took from the gun trunk the guns that were to be used in the act. He told us that years of experience had taught him the best way to pack guns was in common cotton bed blankets; he said that he never allowed two guns to touch each other. Jimmie took complete charge of all the guns that were used in the act and seldom ever allowed anyone else to touch them unless he had a cowboy, that understood guns, help him clean them after they had been used. For they were always polished and the barrels were cleaned perfectly every time they were used, and the guns they had used for years looked like new.

Missie always took a little rest before she dressed for her act, and as we had kept her so busy I think she needed a little extra rest. So after the guns were ready and the ammunition set out, Jimmie took us to the seats he had reserved for us so we could watch the people take their seats, and at the same time Missie could have the rest she had to have in order to do a good act. The minute the doors were opened the people rushed in to the seats like mad. Age seemed to make no difference for they all seemed to be excited and tried to get the front seats except people who stopped to buy reserved seat tickets.

The railroads ran excursions to the show town to accommodate the show patrons for back in the nineties the Buffalo Bill Show was one of the major attractions. People who did not come on the train drove horses for miles, not only bringing their own families but as many of the neighbors as they could. When the seats were filled the canvasman rolled in bales of straw, and scattered it on the ground between the seat section and the arena, and people who were not fortunate enough to get seats could sit on the straw.

Soon the cowboy band began to play *Marching Through Georgia* and the grand entry started. Everyone was thrilled when Buffalo Bill dashed to the front on his spotless white horse. When he got to the front of the arena his horse made a bow to the audience as Buffalo Bill took his broad brimmed hat in his hand and bowed to the applauding people. He said, "I introduce the Buffalo Bill Wild West."

Some times they had the official announcer introduce the different people in groups and after they all rode into the arena and had taken their places then in rode Buffalo Bill wearing his long hair down his back looking like a painted picture as he took his place in front of the group in the arena. Then he led the grand entry out of the back of the arena as fast as they could ride.

After the grand entry the announcer called the different acts in turn. One I remember as being most interesting was the congress of Rough Riders of the World. The Russian Cossacks were the most daring. They wore knee length coats tied in at the waist with a belt that held shells for their guns. They wore queer high turbans and high-topped boots with silver spurs. They rode into the arena standing upon their horses backs, and swinging a long dagger or sword around over their heads. They also carried a sawed off shot gun and as they entered the arena they were singing a dreary song and kept it up until they got to the center of the arena when they suddenly began their fast riding. They rode two horses at a time, by standing with a foot on one horse and one foot on the other. One of the men rode four horses at a time by standing with his feet on the two outside horses with the other two racing between them. Jimmie told us that these tall men had almost perfect health which they needed to stand the hard riding they did every day. Though the Cossacks' riding was most daring one could enjoy it to the fullest extent, for they seemed to enjoy the daredevil stunts themselves.

I liked the cowgirls on their horses. They rode in, and did some fast riding, and put their manage horses through the manage acts. As many as five girls on horseback did the same thing: they threw handkerchiefs on the ground, and with the horses keeping time with the music, they rode near enough to enable the horse to pick up the handkerchief with his teeth. Then the horses turned their heads and gave the handkerchief to the girl on their backs. All of the horses proudly stepped to the front of the arena and made a bow to the audience, for they seemed to like applause as well as the cowgirls themselves. Keeping time with the music, went to their places in the arena and knelt down on their front legs while the girls dismounted gracefully. Then the horses would lie flat on their sides while the girls stood upon them holding their riding whip high up over their head. The horses got upon their feet so gently that their riders could get their feet into their stirrups, and fully mount by the time the horses were on their feet. The girls always rewarded the horses by giving them something they liked to eat.

The South African boomerang throwers were a wonder to every child. The curved wooden missiles were thrown in the war chase by native Australians. The boomerang was made and thrown with great skill.

Johnnie Baker who was billed with the show as "The boy shot of the World," or as "The Young American Marksman." His remarkable fancy shooting had won for him the title. The thing about his act we never forgot was his standing on his head and shooting. When he first put his head to the ground he always got up and picked up a stone and threw it away as if he had been standing on his head on the stone. Then he would try it again, the second time he could stand all right. There always seemed to be a stone in every town right where he wanted to stand on his head.

One reason I was so interested in Johnnie Baker was that I knew how he happened to be with the show. When he was a small boy he ran away from home to be with Buffalo Bill whom he almost worshiped. After having been sent home several times, Buffalo Bill decided to let him go with the show when Johnnie's mother thought that was the best thing to do. At first Cody gave Johnnie the job of shining his boots, but when he found out the lad would really work, he gave him larger responsibilities until he had made himself so valuable that he was made arena director, after several years.

Jimmie found out that Johnnie could shoot, so he gave him a chance to practice. It was not long until Johnnie was shooting so well he was given a place on the program. When the young shooter was quite young he married a lovely girl, and had two little daughters. One of them was just my age, and I had always known about them and was interested in them. One reason was that their mother had died when the younger one was a baby.

The Baker children had been idols of the Wild West camp, as their father had kept them, part of the time with him on the road. Missie often cried when she told about the two little girls going around the camp looking for their mother. The older one remembered her mother and told the younger sister that surely they would find their mother in some town.

Missie's act went very well the day we saw her in Piqua and we thought we had seen her practice it all until she did the very last part, and that was to run and jump over the table that her guns were on, she picked up three glass balls threw them into the air, picked up a gun and broke the balls before they struck the ground. Then she ran as fast as she could to the back of the arena, and just before she ran under the rope that someone held up for her, she turned and gave a funny little step and a kick. To people who knew her, the act would never have been complete without this last little touch.

The last act on the program was always the bucking horses because in wet weather they made the arena muddy and cut up. This made it hard for the other people to work. The show had to go on rain or shine. Someone told me most any horse could be made into a good bucker by slipping the back girth more than four inches back of the front one, and tightening it a little. I tried it the first time I had a chance, and it worked. One of the best buckers I ever saw was a horse that had been driven on a milk wagon, right in New York city. Some playful cowboy had found out he would buck if gurthed like a bucker.

After the bucking horse act the show was over and the band played a lively piece while the thousands of people rushed out from under the big top in a gay mood. The last piece the band played after every performance was always one familiar to most people and a lively one except after the last show of the year and then they played *Home Sweet Home*. The band men were superstitious and thought that if anyone played *Home Sweet Home* before the closing day of the show for the season that something surely would happen that would be unpleasant, or the show would surely have bad business.

After having seen the Wild West Show for the first time we were all tired out and went back to Missie's tent and found her pleased to know we had enjoyed seeing the show so much, for neither my

mother or father had ever seen the show. While we rested and
drank the lemonade that had been sent over from the cook tent,
we watched Jimmie clean the guns, for he cleaned every gun always after it had been used.

Ever so many members of the company came to Missie's tent
to see us. As she loved children and enjoyed telling things about
them, it was quite possible that different members of the company
had heard little things about us. After we visited with the people
who came to see us, some old friends came in to see Missie.

Jimmie knew we had not seen the ticket wagon so he took us
around to the front entrance to where the ticket wagon stood. We
were allowed to go into the ticket wagon where we saw the treasurer counting piles of money that had been taken in for the afternoon performance. After the bills were all paid for the day the treasurer took the remainder of the money to the bank. All of the business for the company was taken care of in the ticket wagons, in
fact it was the office, and a busy place it was. One would wonder
how so much business could be handled in so small a space.

After we had visited with the people in the ticket wagon and
seen all that was going on we went to the ammunition wagon. There
all the guns were kept, as well as the ammunition that was to be
used by all of the members of the company. The cowboys did a lot
of shooting of blank shells, as did the Mexicans and Cossacks, to
say nothing of the shells that were loaded with shot and bullets for
the fancy shooting that Missie, Johnnie Baker and Col. Cody did.
Handling the ammunition was no small task for at that time the
shells were all loaded by hand. So there was an expert in charge of
the wagon who saw to it that the shells were properly loaded. The
glass balls that were used in the acts were made every day by the
man in charge of the wagon. They were very fragile and would break
if packed. Then too they would have taken too much space, for everything had to be packed into as small space as possible. The balls
that were used in the shooting acts were made out of melted glass,
sulphur and resin. They had to be made perfectly or they would
break when thrown into the air before the shot hit them. If they
were too hard they would not break at all. They had molds of

different sizes to make the balls, and it was fun to see the hot mixture sizzle when it was dropped into the cold water, to cool it quickly, so the balls would not be too thick.

The people who wandered about the lot had to be kept a certain distance from the ammunition wagon for there were explosives on hand at all times, so they kept a rope stretched to posts that had been driven into the ground. Many people were anxious to see the shells being loaded and were also interested in seeing the glass balls made.

We saw a mutt dog digging a hole under the ammunition wagon in which to bury a bone. He was a good trouper for he worked all of the time. Every day he would go to the cook's tent, get his dinner, and carry a nice bone back to bury in the hole which he dug. Then he would lie and watch it the rest of the day to make sure no other dog would get it. The next morning, he would go to the ammunition wagon and dig until noon to try to find the bone he had buried the day before. He did not realize the show had been moved to another town during the night, and that the bone he had buried the day before was many miles away. When he got too hungry he would go to the cook tent, get another meal, and take another bone back to the wagon and bury it a little deeper than the one he had buried the day before. By fall he was burying the bones three times as deep as he was tall. Jimmie laughed and said that if that fool dog was a bird dog he would be smart enough to find out his mistake.

There were other interesting things about the dogs that joined the show. In the spring the show would start out with only a dog or two, and by fall they would have a whole troupe of dogs, each one seeming to have his place. Sometimes someone would see a dog in a town and remember what he looked like, and not see the dog for several days. If a dog took a notion to join, he would somehow get on to a flat car and stay until he got better acquainted with some showman that would perhaps take an interest in him, or at least give him a few kind words and a friendly pat on the head. When he got hungry he would follow someone to the show lot, and after he had located the cook's tent he became a regular trouper and perhaps a companion of some lonesome showman.

The Indians kept their eyes open for a dog that would make a good stew, for when they had their dog feasts they wanted a dog that would make a good fat stew. If a dog was unfortunate enough to join out with an Indian, he was likely to meet his fate in a kettle.

I remember that a dog caused a lot of trouble in a southern town. A town boy had seen a certain dog in the Wild West camp, and the next day the boy told the owner of the dog about it. The anxious master of the dog took a train and went to the next town the show went to, and sure enough, there was his dog tied to an Indian dog stake. The owner of the dog had the Indian and the dog both arrested. The town police took both the dog and the Indian to the police station, where a big argument took place. The policeman gave the dog a good slap, to see to whom the lost dog would go. To the man's sorrow the dog ran to the Indian. The dog had made a hit with the Indian and was never made into a stew. He would say, "Hep much good dog, me not kill."

After having seen all of the interesting things about the camp we went into the big dining tent where we ate with all of the show people. Having completed a busy day in camp, with a promise from Missie and Jimmie that they would come to our farm for a short time in the fall, we left them and started home. All the way home and for days after my brother and I planned how we could make a wild west show of our own. So after a night's rest we began to train two pet goats, a calf or two, and a litter of young pigs. We used a grove adjoining the yard and barn lot for our training lot and make-believe arena.

It took only a few days to build some Indian Tepees out of some bark and sticks we found plenty of around a pond not far from our house. This we thought made an ideal setting. The young calves did not mind being lassoed with the clothesline. And the pigs did not run too fast when shot at with arrows we had made out of hickory sticks. The two pet goats let us know they were not made for bucking horses, for each day when they thought they had enough training they tried to chase us up a tree or over a fence. I have no doubt that at the same time we were putting our animals through the course of training other children were doing the same thing. We furnished at least a lot of amusement for our playmates.

We had arranged our show camp as nearly like the Wild West camp as we could, for we had learned that every day in every town the show lot was arranged the same. Otherwise the show people would have spent most of the time trying to find things. Even the Wild West mailman would have had a hard time trying to find everybody. We had very little encouragement from our mother or father at trying to promote our show for they thought shooting at cows pretending they were buffalo was rather a silly play, so most of our achievements were original with us, but were enjoyed by the children in the neighborhood, for most of them had never seen a show and believed all we told them to be true.

In The Western Girl.

26
BUFFALO BILL SENDS GUN

DURING THE SUMMER of 1895 Buffalo Bill sent us the gun he had promised to send, and I shall never forget the day it arrived. It was nailed up in a wooden box, and to our surprise, when my father opened the box, the gun was a Winchester repeating .44 calibre, Model 1860 size. There was a lot of brass shells to go with the gun. Father got a new board about three feet long and set it up by the side of a tree in the woods. He took a ripe pokeberry off a bush that was near, and made a little spot on the upper end of the board. Then we all took turns trying out the gun.

Later mother proved to be the best shot of the family. If she saw a chicken hawk she would run and get the gun, and often brought him down. The gun did not shoot far enough to kill them every time but it was not very long until the hawks seemed to know better than to come near our chickens. They did not like the sound of the gun.

We had many ducks on the pond, and the snapping turtles would catch them for food. I have seen my mother stand on the bank of the pond with the gun in her hand, and when a snapper got a duck by the foot, she would shoot the turtle before he got the duck under the water. Usually the duck was injured so badly he died but we then had the turtle for a meal.

When mother wanted to kill a chicken she got the one she wanted out by itself, then she shot its head off. Many times she would see a rabbit coming through the orchard, and call for someone to bring her the gun, so she could keep her eyes upon the

173

rabbit. We usually had our rabbit for dinner. During the hunting season we seldom went away from home hunting. Mother said she had better luck staying right at home. When hunters started shooting, the birds and rabbits would come to the orchard for protection, then mother could watch for the game in comfort.

One day Missie and Jimmie went hunting. It was near the end of the season and they came home without even seeing a bird or a rabbit. While they were gone my mother had shot two nice young rabbits in the orchard, my father cleaned them quickly and cooled the warm meat, and they were all cooked and ready to serve by the time the hunters were ready to eat.

The gun was quite new to the family as yet when my father tried his luck by shooting snakes that came to the barn in search of milk from the cows. He was not too good a shot and always said snakes were the very hardest thing to kill and if he missed he would say, "I know Annie could not have hit the snakes I shot at and missed." One time I saw him shoot a black snake in two and was surprised to see both pieces run away.

Once my brother and I were left alone with a housekeeper, when I was nine years old. We were to be alone several days so we set up the wild west show and gave the animals a little extra training. Then we started out into the orchard to try to locate some new animals to train. To our surprise we came across a nest of baby snakes. Our first thought was to try to kill them with a stick. We listened to their funny squeaky noise for a minute, then we ran to the house and had a hard time to convince the housekeeper that it was safe for us to take the gun to kill the snakes. At last she decided to go with us to see if we really had seen something to shoot. While my brother and I were arguing about who was to do the shooting, the mother snake opened her mouth and all the baby snakes ran down her throat. The snake ran down a hole that was near, and we had let her get away. To this day we can dig up a good argument as to who let the snakes get away.

Missie was always interested in all the things her family were interested in doing. She always wanted to hear from us and we told in detail about the show we tried to produce and the shooting we did with the old gun. All that it took to get plenty of shells for the gun was to write a letter and tell what we had shot and Jimmie would soon figure out how soon we needed shells.

In Missie's childhood they had not had toys and dolls to play with and not much time to play for when she was not much more than a baby she had taken care of her two younger sisters and her only brother. She had to work so hard that she enjoyed seeing her nieces and nephews have a happy normal life that children are entitled to. Somehow my mother understood and wrote her very often telling her of all of the doings on our farm, and she was always interested and enjoyed doing little things to help make life more enjoyable for us.

One of the things she did was to send mother her dresses as she wanted new ones, and mother could make them over for me and sometimes the material would be heavy enough and a good color for a suit for my brother. As I grew a little older she would tell me that if I would rip up a garment she would give it to me for my mother to make over into a good dress or a coat. I learned to sew partly because I was interested to see how things had been put together, and as I ripped the garments I was interested in saving the thread of different colors, and if I could save a piece long enough to sew with, I was delighted and wound it on a piece of cardboard or an empty spool, each color separately. When Missie came home one time I showed her my sewing box. I am sure nothing ever pleased her more, and she told me of how hard it had been for her to get even a little thread to sew with when she was a little girl. She also told me of some of the hardships of her childhood and I felt so much sympathy for her that always after that we seemed to grow closer every time we were together. This relationship was noticed by other members of the family (not my father and mother) but my aunts and cousins and they never had the same friendly feeling for me they had always shown. Missie explained it to me and all of the rest of her life I tried in my own way to make up to her for the pleasure she had missed as a child. She seemed to enjoy seeing me do the things she had wanted to do and could not. It was not always easy for me to please my beloved aunt for my mother had different ideas at times and it meant I had to choose between the two. Usually I chose to please Missie for I felt that in my mother's childhood she had not been deprived of quite as much as her sister had been.

After Missie found out that I was interested in sewing she was always looking for things that I could make for myself. As I learned to make things that she could wear she bought material and patterns and often sent them to me to make for her. She was very exacting and hard to please, but seemed to have patience to try to teach me to make garments as neat as she herself made. I think she felt that if I could please her I could always do sewing for her that was hard to get anyone else to do.

Every spring and fall everything was gone over and Missie decided what she would not want to use again, and she would make a bundle and send to my mother. In the package she would put some new things that she had been able to buy. There were always spools of thread for my sewing, and I felt the new thread was a treasure and that not a piece of it should be wasted when sewing for my dolls or myself, and to this day I often think of how much Missie tried to save because of her early experience. Other members of the family seemed to think she was simply cranky or queer and did not seem to be able to tolerate her exactness, so I think she appreciated my understanding her. It was a great pleasure to me when I could please her, and knew I had her approval of anything I did. As I grew older I was always trying to think of something I could make for her that she could use, or of something I could do to please her that no one else even knew of.

The house in Nutley, New Jersey, was too much of a responsibility for Missie and Jimmie after a year or two. They decided to travel a few more years so they stored the furniture and rented the house but later sold it, and never went back to Nutley to live except to board, but for a good many years they called Nutley their home.

The fall of 1894 the letter came that Missie and Jimmie would spend several months with us on the farm. There was great rejoicing and Mother began to prepare the house to be as comfortable as possible. New straw ticks were filled and the feathers that had been stored in bags or barrels in the corn crib to dry were put into new ticking and put on the top of the freshly filled straw ticks. The new rag carpet was put down in the living room, the old was scrubbed and tacked down in the bedroom that Missie and Jimmie were to occupy. The kitchen stove was moved from the summer kitchen into the winter quarters and it seemed that nothing was left undone to make the coming of the famous couple a pleasant reception. I thought everything had been finished when suddenly my mother began to tell me not to ask my aunt and uncle, the minute they arrived, how long they intended to stay. It seemed I always had done it, but Mother thought I was old enough to act like a grown-up. My brother and I had been given a few new instructions as to how we should behave, now that I we were five and seven.

It was a happy day for my family when it was time for the guests to arrive. My father had the driving horse brushed until he fairly glistened in the fall sunlight. We could not go along to Versailles, the town two and one-half miles away, for there was too much baggage to bring back from the train. I do not remember what I wore that day, but my brother wore the waist with the ruffled collar and cuffs, and pants made out of a skirt of one of Missie's shooting costumes, and there was the little Eton jacket that had been made out of the blouse waist to match. Mother delighted in dressing my brother up to look like a city kid and he not knowing any better enjoyed it until he was old enough to notice how other farm boys dressed. I think it was because she enjoyed making his clothes.

When father drove up with the guests, mother, my brother and I were waiting at the gate and greeted them, and the very first chance I had I asked Missie how long they intended to stay, the very thing I had been told not to do, but I was so anxious to have them stay a long time. I am sure my aunt understood for I never heard that she told my mother. If she ever had, I felt sure I would have heard about it.

It seemed I was as intimately familiar with my aunt's real character during her visit at this time as I ever was during her whole life. It was quite unusual that I should be able to comprehend her fundamental characteristics at such an age. Little did I think I was building a fast friendship and an admiration that would develop into a devotion that could be recognized by strangers later in life. Over a period of thirty years the devotion I had for both Missie and Jimmie grew until at the end of their lives newspaper people came to me from far to hear what I thought about writing a story of their lives.

Presents were in the bag for us all, and Missie had brought my brother Lee and me striped stockings and stocking caps. We wore them to school the next day and mine looked all right to the old fashioned country children, but Lee's made him miserable, for the boys called him girl baby and on the way home he hid his stocking cap in the bushes and I wore out the stockings, and did not seem to mind being called funny because the other children did not wear different colored stockings. I think the striped hose were brand new even in the cities and Missie thought she was bringing us something we would like. Another thing she gave me was material for a new dress and Mother made it without a collar but low in the neck, but the girls told me they could see my craw, and that was almost too much for me to bear, so I only wore the dress places my mother went.

It was only a few days until I came home from school and was told I might stay out of school and go with my aunt to visit my grandmother.

We started early one morning to drive to North Star to stay a few days. It was during this long drive that I first began to hear from my aunt about her childhood, and how my grandmother had raised her family after the father had died, leaving her to care for the family alone.

While I was at grandmother's I slept in an old cord bed upstairs and my aunt took from a drawer in the big walnut chest the family Bible and showed me where my name had been written when I was born. She also told me that her maiden name had been Phoebe Annie Mozee, but that all of the rest of the family had thought it was Moses. It did not mean much to me at that time, but a few years later my mother went to show me in the same Bible where my name was written and she was surprised to find that someone had tried to erase the name Moses and in its place write Mozee. Our visit was soon over and we were on our way home, and it had all seemed so wonderful to have Missie all to myself.

One of the last photographs.

27

MISSIE TELLS AN INDIAN STORY

INDIAN LORE was another thing Missie loved and knew a great deal about. The Algonquins had been the most numerous in the southern section of Ohio. The most prominent tribes such as the Ottawas, Potawatomies, and Chippewas, came down from the lake region. The Miami came from the Maumee River. In the valley of the Scioto were the Shawnees whose wandering disposition was shown by their various migrations.

These tribes became warlike when the white men encroached upon their territory, and the period of warfare in the Southern part of Ohio lasted over forty years.

Then the calumet pipe of peace was smoked, and the treaty of Greenville was signed in 1795. This was a grand tribute to General Wayne, and was a striking pledge of peace and good will. The chiefs and warriors who gave their hand to General Wayne at Greenville were never known to fight against the United States again.

The tribes that sent representatives to sign the treaty at Greenville were the Potawatomies, Wyandottes, Shawnees, Miamis, Chippewas, Ottawas, Weas, Prankerahaws, Kickapoos, and the Kaskarans. In all there were about eleven hundred Indians, not including the friendly tribes that were protected by the government. It was not until 1814 that all the hostile tribes signed the treaty of peace.

The early settlers who came to Darke County could tell many tales of frontier life. It was no doubt from these settlers Missie gained her knowledge of Indian life.

After my first visit alone with my aunt, I wished that it would be possible to have her go on forever telling stories of her life and of the Indian life of America.

When we arrived home Uncle Frank said he had a letter from Buffalo Bill telling him it was time to go on to New York to get ready for the show in the Madison Square Garden. This meant their visit would be over in a few days.

Mother hurried to put the last finishing touches on some dresses she was making for Missie. This took some time, for if there ever was anyone particular about their clothes, it was Missie. When she was in Paris she saw some dresses she liked, and wanted mother to copy them, which she did. Every seam had to be finished just right, and everything had to match perfectly. It was very hard to get anyone to sew for her that could please her, and mother always did her best and Missie seemed to like to have her to do some sewing for her when she was near enough.

One day when Jimmie did not seem to be busy, he made Lee and I very happy. He said that if we did exactly as we were told, he would teach us to shoot. We made the promise, and he took us to an open field where we started our first shooting lesson. We were not as good shots the first day as we were later. We were too excited to do our best but Jimmie seemed to know that, for he let us do a lot of practicing. Ammunition was plentiful for Buffalo Bill had promised us all the shells we wanted.

By the time I was ten years old, we were trusted to take the gun out to kill rats and redheads that stole the cherries. Father had put a pole high up in the very tallest cherry tree, for the redheads always lit on the highest branch first. We could not shoot them in the tree for if we did the shot would injure the tree. The gun we used was a repeating Winchester, a forty-four caliber, model eighteen sixty-six.

I never had an accident with the gun though I very nearly did. A friend of mother's was shooting at mark one day and the mark happened to be tin cans set in a row on the top of a fence. We took turns setting up the mark, and it was the friend's turn to set the mark. While I was waiting for her to get through, I set the trigger which was forbidden until time to shoot. One thing that saved me perhaps from shooting the best friend my mother had, was the fact that I had been taught to hold the gun properly, and that was with the muzzle of the gun always down, four inches from the right foot.

That taught me to observe always the rules to the strictest letter. I had a good fright. When my friend asked me if I had an accident, I said that I had just tried to scare her, but I was the one that had the scare. I decided then and there that there would be fewer accidents if everyone observed the rules for shooting.

Jimmie thought he had taught us a few things about shooting. The one thing that he wanted to make sure of was that we would know how to handle a gun properly and have enough practice that we would not have an accident. He taught us never to point even a toy gun at anyone or at anything we did not want to shoot. He always said that it is always the gun that is not loaded that kills someone.

Not knowing how important it was that I learn to handle a gun properly, I did so because I wanted to be obedient and thought it fun at the time. In after years I realized and appreciated what a kindness my uncle had done me during the early years of my life. Many years later when I could go hunting with Missie and Jimmie I never remember of them having to correct me for the way in which I handled a gun. It seemed second nature to me to use firearms although because of being nearsighted I never cared to try to do trap shooting, and never became a very good shot in the field.

One cold fall evening Missie and Jimmie started to tell all about what happened to the show people and the stock during the winter. For a good many years the show wintered in Bridgeport, Connecticut. In winter the equipment was all put in first class shape. Each year by the time the season was over it would seem as though most everything needed repairing, even though things were kept in the best shape possible during the traveling season.

The show never stopped for bad weather when the season came to travel. In some towns the show lot would be a regular mud hole before the show was ready to start. If the lot was at all low the heavy hauling that was necessary to get the equipment on the lot would cut it up. Missie told about how at times she had to stand on a bale of straw to dress for her act. People who wanted to see the show did not seem to mind going through the rain and mud if they wanted to see the show, for they had a chance to see a show only once in two or three years.

Bad weather was hard on the equipment for the mud made the wagons harder to pull and more harnesses broke, and more wagons wore out.

One of the interesting things they did in winter quarters was to mend the big top, as the main tent was called. It was a tremendous task to handle all of the canvas. Some years the whole tent had to be replaced at a great cost. All of the seats had to be repaired, the broken ones had to be replaced, and they all had to be painted so that they looked like new. The dining tent benches and tables had to be replaced and painted as well as all of the wagons. On the wagons that went in parade they used a great deal of gold paint so they could be seen a long way off. Most of the wagons went in the parade except the cook and ammunition wagons, and they were busy places during the time the parade was on the streets.

One of the most responsible people with the show was the boss canvasman, who saw that the tents were taken down after the show was over at night and put up the next day in time for the show to start. Naturally the man in charge of the tents was on hand in winter quarters to see that the work was done properly and that the canvas would be in shape to last the next season.

The cook's wagon and the dining tent were the first to be taken down every night when traveling. As soon as the evening meal was served the cooking equipment was taken down and packed in the big wagon and put on the train. Then the cookhouse men were through for the day. They were the first ones up and out in the morning so as to have breakfast ready for the people.

Some of the work of taking down and putting up the canvas was done by men who went with the show and they were called canvasmen. They always had to pick up some town men to help handle the big piles of canvas. In those days the ten stakes were driven by hand with heavy wooden mallets, and each day town men were paid to help. Another very important man that was sure to be in winter quarters to supervise, was the manager of the reserved seats as well as the seats along the sides of the arena. If just one brace was to slip from its place when the seats were up many people would be hurt, and the company would have had the damages to pay.

The man who took care of the lights and torches had a real job, also, for he had to see that lights were going everywhere one was needed. Over a period of years they had tried different kinds of lights, and found that the oil was the most satisfactory. It took a great number of lights to light the camp. It was like lighting a small town. The lights had to be good to enable the shooters to see objects thrown into the air. When the show train pulled into a town a town officer was to meet the train and the man in charge of lights with the show. Together they would lay out the route from the train to the show ground, and put an oil torch at the corners where they were to turn. The torch was set on the corner of the sidewalk that they were to turn around. Even the animals learned to find the lot. Horses often got loose at the cars, and without anyone going with them they could find their way to the show grounds.

Horses in winter were given the best care, and some of them trained to do acts in the arena. The steers that were used to draw the covered wagon were sometimes sold in the fall and other ones brought from Cody's ranch to take their places.

One experience after another was told that perfect fall evening and somehow as a child I felt it was such a privilege to listen to all of the interesting things my aunt and uncle had to tell, and I felt like I could write a story for each time I heard them tell the true stories. It seemed as if the time was too short and that bedtime came too quickly.

One experience Missie told happened when they had been in a small town in Tennessee. The railroads had run excursions into the town from the show. People had driven in many miles from the country. One woman had driven an old spring wagon a good many miles, and had brought along several children. One, a sick baby, died on her lap during the afternoon performance. The mother took the dead child and laid her in the old spring wagon, covered her up, and went back to see the show. Missie heard about it after her act was over, and was at the wagon when the mother came to go home. The poor woman told Missie it would take her most of the night to get back to the rest of her family. She said she could bury the child any time, but she may never have a chance to see another show in all her life, so the little performer's heart was touched and her mind went back to the time when her own mother had death visit her home with so little money to help out with. Missie, as one who knew her would expect, slipped a ten dollar bill into the hand of the worried mother, that would help to bury the little soul.

A lot of poor children were able to see the show because Missie often raised up the side of the tent somewhere back of the seats and let them in, for they could not see the show any other way. When the show was in a town where there was an orphan's home Missie would tell Cody about it and say that if he would let the children in free, she would treat them all to ice cream and candy. Sometimes they would have several hundred children from a home. Missie said she could always shoot better that day for having had the pleasure of helping to entertain the children.

The busy little Missie was always looking for children to whom she could give something to make their day a little brighter. She often found a boy on the lot early in the morning and asked him if he thought his mother could do a little laundry for her; If the boy thought she could, Missie would start out with the boy, letting him carry the bundle of clothes to be done. There were not many laundries in those days that would do the work in one day. If it were a clear day a woman could wash and iron all of the clothes Missie had in one day.

One time she thought she found a boy whose mother could do the work and the boy told her that his mother needed the money. They started out and she asked how far it was to where he lived. The boy told her, "Just a little way." They walked ten or twelve blocks and then Missie inquired how much farther and the boy's answer was the same as before. "Oh! just a little farther." The boy wanted his mother to have the work so badly that Missie was encouraged to keep on going. When she got to where the laundry was to be taken, she found she had walked three miles and that it was almost noon. She agreed that the family did need the little money she would pay for the work so left it to be done, wondering if she would get it back in time for the show train to leave at night. But sure enough the boy was on hand with the bundle of clean clothes that were done to please even the particular little Missie.

Jimmie often said he thought that Missie tried to find all of the pathetic poor little waifs on the lot. I can understand why she was always looking out for such children and feeling sorry for them. It was because of her childhood experiences that she never could forget. I have been with her when she saw children poorly dressed and she would say, "I wonder if I looked like that when I was a child." Then she would try to explain to me how hard times had been for her mother.

The Author shooting for the pleasure of some Indians.

28
SHOW OPENS IN MADISON SQUARE GARDEN, 1898

AFTER A HURRIED TRIP for a visit to my home in the fall of 1898, Missie and Jimmie went to Newark, New Jersey, where they spent most of the winter in the Continental Hotel, owned by Lewis E. Cook who had been advance agent for the Buffalo Bill show for a number of years. In April as usual the show opened in the Madison Square Garden. War was in the air and Cody once more felt the patriotism glow, and somehow the eyes of the public were turned to him in wonder as to what move he would make. At Missie's suggestion the management of the Wild West turned the Garden over to the orphans of New York City for one day. A gay day it must have been, the Cuban flag was carried along by the side of the American flag, and the Garden rang with cheers as did the arena, at all of the performances all that year. Artillerymen and cavalry had been added to the program along with two cannons, to bring in a vivid way to the public the sense of war again. There was talk about Teddy Roosevelt's friendship with Cody and he did offer his services to the government along with Teddy.

Cody had not forgotten what the Spaniards tried to do to his show in Madrid, Spain, when his cowboys told them they did not like their national sport. The never failing advertising man John Burk said, "Cody could make Spain bow down with thirty thousand Indians, if he had a chance." It was not Cody's fault that he did not go to Cuba.

Late in August, 1898, at the Trans-Mississippi Exposition, in celebrating the Winning of the West, Col. Cody was Nebraska's

189

most famous son, and August the thirty-first was celebrated as
Cody Day, and more than thirty thousand people saw the show that
day, the largest audience since the Chicago World's Fair. Fifteen
years before the Buffalo Bill Show had been born in Omaha, and
many of the people who saw the show that first day came to see
the vast changes that had taken place. One of the features was
the shooting act of Annie Oakley. Johnnie Baker was another solo
attraction, and the Congress of Rough Riders of the World, carrying the flags of all nations. Then the war was over and sixteen of
Roosevelt's Rough Riders were added, and some Hawaiians, Fili-
pinos and Cubans. Neither had they seen the added attractions in
the sideshow, namely the mind readers, jugglers, midgets, and the
fat boy, giant, and fat girl.

Some of the patrons did like the circus attractions, but the cowboys and the Mexicans and Indians had a feeling that they were
there first and the sideshow did not belong to them. The cowboys
did welcome the rough riders and went into the production of San
Juan Hill with the Cubans to help them out, and made an interesting reproduction of the battle.

That year father sold the farm and bought one not far from
Greenville. Missie had all of her belongings stored in Nutley and
she wanted to have the huge trunks and boxes where she could get
into them when she liked, so she had them sent to our new farm.
Then the fall of 1899 Missie and Jimmie came and had some good
hunting. We all liked that farm. There were cherry trees to attract
the redheads in the spring and Lee and I could take turns shooting
the old forty-four. Mother had a good orchard to shoot rabbits in.
Father had plenty to keep him busy. The dog had plenty of old log
buildings to kill rats around while they were being torn down. When
Missie and Jimmie came they made new friends and beside the
hunting, they liked to show the neighbors their new shooting
stunts.

In 1900 the show came to Greenville, Ohio, and we were all so
delighted to see our friends and Missie and Jimmie. The show train
got in very early in the morning and was on the siding on the tracks
not far from the railroad station. We knew we would find Missie in

her car early in the morning so father took my best girl friend, Ethel Cox, to the train and Jimmie asked us if we would like to go in the parade. He probably wanted to get rid of us. We assured him that we would like to ride in parade, thinking we were going to ride in a big fine looking wagon, but instead he put us in the dirty old stage-coach with some Indian Squaws, and we were scared to pieces, but we were game and never said a thing, half ashamed because the stagecoach was so old.

The show went well and after Missie's act, Jimmie told her to linger just a second, when out from the reserved section stepped Charlie Anderson, one of the town lawyers, with something under his arm, a token of love and affection the people of her hometown had for the famous little star. It was a silver loving cup. That was the only time I ever saw Missie cry in the arena. It was more than she could stand to think her hometown had loved her so much. The family did not have much time with her that day, so after she could get away from the crowd of friends who wanted a word with her, we all went to the hotel and had a restful time and a visit with Missie and Jimmie.

The shock of a lifetime came in the fall of 1901 when the news was flashed all over the world, that the Buffalo Bill Show had gone into a head on collision near Wheeling, West Virginia, and that Annie Oakley had been nearly killed. Missie had been thrown from her bed against a trunk and her spine had been injured and the nerve shock was so great that her hair turned white in seventeen hours.

One hundred and ten head of horses were killed, and as they carried Missie by the suffering animals she felt so sorry of them, which partly caused the shock. She suffered injuries from which she never fully recovered.

The show traveled in two sections, and one section had passed the signal station and the operator thought the whole show had gone by, and he signaled a freight from Washington into the last section of the Wild West train.

All the years that Missie and Jimmie had traveled they had never been in an accident, nor had they ever had any sort of an accident with a gun. The show was to have closed in Wheeling the next day, and they were to retire from the Wild West that season. It was some months before they were able to travel and come to our farm where they wanted to have a rest.

My father met Missie and Jimmie at the train and I never shall forget how bad Mother felt when she saw Missie's white hair. The white hair was very becoming to her though, when one got used to seeing it, but the white eyelashes and the eyebrows left no protection for her eyes from the light and sun: All the rest of her life she had to color them, and she felt it was such a bother.

After a major operation to correct a torn kidney, Missie was more like herself and wanted to do something, to try to forget the experience of the wreck.

Langsdown McCormic wrote the *Western Girl*, and Missie starred in it. The play had a good run in New York, but when they took it on the road they found the scenery had been built too large for the average theatre, and they only had a short run, playing to good houses where they went. Missie closed the show and sent the scenery to our farm to be stored, thinking it might be rebuilt and used sometime. When father had the scenery stored a small piece was overlooked and left on the wagon that they had used to haul it. Mother discovered that the material was good linen. The scenery was never rebuilt, but instead the linen was used by the family and friends, after the paint was all washed out. They made towels, table cloths, dresser scarves, and all kinds of things out of it.

Along with the scenery Missie sent Prince her fine saddle horse to be cared for at our farm. Her saddle and trappings came too. It was not long before we rode Prince as spirited as he was. We had the beautiful horse some years and Missie enjoyed riding him when she had a chance. We had a sad day when one damp day father turned him out for exercise and he slipped on straw and fell and broke his leg. Grandmother was visiting us at the time. We all had a good cry and no one felt as bad as father, when he got his good neighbor Abe Arnold to come and shoot the suffering animal. Abe had liked Prince and he said he never had shot an animal that made him feel so bad.

Missie and Jimmie were wonderful about the death of Prince, and never felt that it was father's fault.

After Missie closed the *Western Girl*, she was in Nutley, New Jersey, with friends. Jimmie was in the south attending a big shooting match. One morning the story started in Chicago. Big headlines "Annie Oakley Steals a Negro's Trousers, and Sells Them to Buy Morphine." Other papers carried the headlines, "The Downfall of Annie Oakley, She Steals a Negro's Trousers and Sells Them to Buy Morphine."

Needless to say that numerous papers had printed the lie, but on the same page contradicted the story. Jimmie rushed to Missie and they employed a law firm in New York, and at once sued fifty-three newspapers that had printed the article as true. They were eight years fighting the cases. Clarence Darrow, then a young lawyer, combined the fifty-three papers, but Missie won every case. Missie had cost the fighting newsmen over eight hundred thousand dollars. The newsmen had sent lawyers all over the world where Missie had been to try to get evidence against her character. One man came to Greenville, Ohio. When the people found what he was there for, he was not allowed to stay overnight. They had not left a stone unturned to get evidence against Missie and I was with her part of the time she was prosecuting her cases, and I know the trials were hard for her to endure. She would often fast and pray for days before a trial date. She said her mind was clearer when she got on the witness stand. In the cross examinations the lawyers tried every way they could think of to win a point.

A letter from Col. Cody:

Luton, London
Sept. 1st, 1903

Frank E. Butler
New York

Dear Frank:
The article you sent me does Annie as well as myself
a great injustice. Let me know your lawyers' opinion,

and what you propose doing.

Very truly,

W. F. Cody

My best wishes to Annie.

During the trials when Missie found she would be around New York, she had all of the trunks and boxes that had been stored at our farm in Ohio sent on to her but they never arrived, and the railroad had to make a settlement for the valuable things that had been stolen. The money she received could not in the least way pay for her treasured things that had come from all over the world. However, seven or eight years later a box car was discovered in Brooklyn, with some of the things still in boxes; some were damaged beyond repair, there were two paintings and three pictures of Missie on horseback that could be reframed. She gave them to my mother later and I still have them, and treasure them because Missie enjoyed them.

It was not until 1902 that the word came that the good friend, Nate Salsbury, had died after so many years of suffering. It was with regret that they gave him up. Cody had always been able to take problems to his one time partner, and he missed Salsbury more than anyone could imagine. Missie had always kept a photograph of Mrs. Salsbury and two of her children, and one of the first things that came out of her trunk every day was the framed photograph. She placed it on her table in the tent and told everyone that was the wife and children of the man who made Buffalo Bill and Annie Oakley.

When Jimmie was traveling he seldom came home without a bit of poetry he had written on the train. I liked "Mamie's Christmas Tree." He told me how on his way to catch a train in down town New York, he was caught in a heavy shower. He stepped under an awning. Soon he was joined by a small boy dragging a Christmas tree, larger than himself. The boy was followed by a mongrel dog that seemed to have a property interest in the tree. Jimmie said, "Hello kid, I see you're going to have a Christmas tree," to which the boy replied, "Aw, go on, this ain't fer me, it's fer me sister, Mamie, ain't it Jimmie?" The dog responded by jumping up and wagging his tail, as long as a rabbit's. Jimmie said it was not hard to draw the Christmas comedy from the pair.

MAMIE'S CHRISTMAS TREE

Jimmie an me's
Got a swell Christmas tree
Staked and hid out in the way,
Jimmie s me pup
But you gamble he's up
And that he stands in on the play.

We're goin' to buy
All the prettiest things
That a feller can find on Broadway.
And we'll give little Mame,
That's me sister's name,
The whiz of a Christmas day.

The kid ain't so pert
Since the day she got hurt
But she's game and don't never cry.
That's why me mazoo
Is down in me shoe
And not spent for no sinkers nor pie.

We're goin' to rastle
The pretties things,
That's Jimmie and me,
And no Avenoo kid
Can come in for a bid
Nor a peek at me Mame's Christmas tree.

Her stocking's too small
And won't do at all
To hold all the things dat night,

But ders one o me mudder's
Dat beats all de oders
And filled up will look out of sight.
Me mudder once said,
Course 'fore she was dead,
Dat she'd look down on Mame and me
I hope from her place
She can see Mame's face
When the kid gets a peek at dat tree.

About this time Missie's dominant character was displayed when she was with us in Ohio. She decided to have some work done on the family cemetery near Yorkshire. She had a cement wall put around the plot and the graves filled and grass seed put in. At the cemetery near Brock, where her brother had two children and his family buried, there had never been markers at the graves. Uncle John had gone to Oklahoma to live many years before, and Missie thought she would settle the dispute of the family once and for always, so she had markers put at the children's graves and spelled their names, Johnnie and Cletis Mozee. Years after when my uncle had come back to visit and went to the cemetery and found the markers had been placed there they were pleased, but he was mad and wanted to have the names changed, but my good-natured Aunt Laury persuaded him to not do it, for after all, what was the use. In later years when Dr. Howard Moses, of Salina, Kansas, began looking up the family records to get data for a book, *The Moses Family*, he found no one in Pennsylvania who spelled the name Mozee, and after several years correspondence with him I am convinced, that the story of Missie's early childhood must be true, when the children had made a hateful rhyme calling her Moses Poses.

Dr. Howard Moses sent me a greeting card with the picture of the Moses anvil and the date on it was 1643, the verse read.

In the old Colonial days, in Plymouth the land of the
   Pilgrims,

Working day after day through times of trial and
    privation
Resounded the clang of the anvil
Of John Moses, the shipwright of Plymouth.
The anvil, preserved as an heirloom, passed down
    through ten generations
Perpetrates the oldest industrial relic from Colonial
    days
Now rests in a New York museum,
Fort Ticonderoga, the honored.

When Missie knew she would not live long she bought from her brother two graves in the Brock cemetery between the two children and she wanted to be buried there, and later Jimmie told me he would choose the same spot. All this goes to show she was a strong willed soul, all because of childhood experiences.

Missie and Jimmie both had missed having a better education than they had, and were much interested in seeing every young person get all of the education they could, and helped in a generous way to see that they did. Missie, with hardly a grade school education and Jimmie with less, were always at work to improve themselves. After they had hobnobbed with Kings and Queens all over Europe, and with people in all walks of life in America, they said that it would have been easier for them had they had a better education.

During the time we lived in New York City Missie and Jimmie gave some shooting exhibitions for the Remington Arms Company and the Union Metallic Cartridge Company. One or two of the exhibitions were in Ohio and we went to visit our family. Jimmie liked buttermilk, and as he was drinking a glass of his favorite he said that a pig in Ohio was better off than a gentleman in New York.

My brother did not like to do any kind of farm work, and Jimmie wrote "Waiting for the Spring."

WAITING FOR THE SPRING
De plow am in de tool house,

De mule am in de stall;
De field am full of stubbles
Where the shivering rabbits crawl.

I want to hear de bluebirds
Up in de tree tops sing,
I want to get to working,
'Ca'se I'se waitin' for de Spring.

De clouds am gray and frowning
De old cow chews her cud
She longs for de pastures
When de peach trees bud.

De trees am still as naked
As a baby jay bird's wing.
I long to say, "Get up dar mule,"
I'se waitin' fer de Spring.

Col. Cody was helpless to plan ahead very far and had lost heavily, so in 1908 after Bailey died his interest had been sold to Major Lilly, better known as Pawnee Bill. I shall never forget one morning in New York when Missie and I were downtown shopping, and we dropped in the Wild West office to see Col. Cody. He actually cried tears when he saw Missie, and said "Annie, I have come to this." His heart was broken. Cody knew that with the new owner, came Pawney Bill's Far East; and that meant pageantry of pomp and a procession of trained elephants and other animals. Cody did not like the Hindu fakers, and the Japanese dancers.

The last time I saw Col. Cody was in Detroit with the 101 ranch in 1916 during the summer. He gave his last public appearance November 11, 1916, after more than thirty years of fame and fortune. And January 10, 1917, he died. As the funeral procession wound through the streets of Denver, two cowboys led a riderless white horse and several more walked. A year later Major Burk died of a broken heart for if there ever was a hero worshipper it was he, and when Cody died there seemed no more work for the Major and he died. He wanted to be with Cody.

Missie loved to give exhibitions for charity, and when she had a chance, she could shoot as well as she had in her younger days. For several years Missie and Jimmie went to Florida and spent the winter in Leesburg, or to Pinehurst, North Carolina, where she did some shooting at the gun club or hunting in the field.

One rainy day Jimmie came into our living room with, "What A Little Bird Said."

WHAT A LITTLE BIRD SAID
I was sitting at my window,
Just at the close of day;
When a little bird lit on the sill,
And these words he seemed to say.

Don't waste your brightest hours,
Pining for things beyond your reach;
Live up to the golden rule,
And practice what you preach.

Life is like a game of cards,
In which we pass our stand;
Sometimes the stake is a true heart,
Oft times it's but a hand.

Sometimes we take in the trick,
Which we should have past;
But if you play your cards for all they're worth
You're bound to win at last.

Jimmie loved poetry and from time to time he wrote verses for his friends.

As Missie joined the young Buffalo Show.

29
JOINS YOUNG BUFFALO SHOW

WHILE WE WERE in Leesburg for the winter of 1912 Jimmie had a letter from V. C. Seavers, owner of the Young Buffalo Wild West show. Seavers had made Missie and Jimmie an offer to travel with his Wild West the year before and they had gone to try to build up the business for their friend because he was not a showman and was in danger of losing all the money he had in the show. The offer Seavers made Missie interested her, for she thought she would enjoy traveling again. They said that I might travel with them that season, which I did. In the spring we went to Peoria, Ill., where we joined the show. The show was a combination of Wild West and Far East. I would not have taken a lot for my experience that season. I tried about everything there was to do around the camp, for life gets rather dull even with a show if there is nothing to do. I played the calliope, sometimes, rode in parade or in the grand entry. Often I took money at the candy stand cash register, sold reserved seat tickets, at the gate at the seats. Once I tried playing *Home Sweet Home*, on one of the band instruments, when the band boys were taking a rest in the afternoon. I never tried that again, for they almost mobbed me, because of the superstition they had that it was bad luck to play *Home Sweet Home* before the closing day of the show for the season.

Rube Delroy was not a clown but may as well have been. The only difference was that he was dressed like a rube instead of a clown. Curtis Liston, who did a shooting with the show, would throw Rube's straw hat into the air and I would shoot at it with a

201

twelve gauge shot gun. In a few days the hat started to fall to pieces, then Rube wanted me to buy him a new hat.

Something different was always happening. One morning as I came to the lot I met a cowboy carrying something in his hat. As I came near him he showed me a nest of baby rabbits. He had been on the lot soon after the canvas men were, and found the nest and knew if he did not rescue the young rabbits they would be killed. The cowboy gave the bunnies enough warm milk to keep them going all day and stayed on the lot until after the lot was cleared, then he put the nest near a bush, then stayed near enough so the mother rabbit could locate the nest. He called like a baby rabbit and waited, and sure enough the mother came and claimed her family. The next day he told me he had made a study of small animals and he knew the mother rabbit would come back.

Another morning as I came to the lot I saw a crowd of people gathered around someone and I went to see what had happened. Here it was Brownie the keeper and owner of a small elephant that worked in the Far East. Brownie had gone into the sideshow tent and as he passed the big elephants one of them picked him up and threw him the length of the tent and he lit on a candy stand. He had not been hurt badly, but no one could think what had happened that made the big elephant throw the man, except a few days before Brownie had had an argument with the keeper of the troupe of elephants.

One Sunday morning we were late getting into the town we were going to show in the next day. As the show trains have to give way to all regular trains, our train was shifted on to a siding several miles from the town. The train master told us that we would more than likely be there an hour. Missie looked across the field and saw a nice looking farmhouse. She called to Lon, our porter, and asked him if he would like to go over and see if he could buy some fresh milk and a chicken or two. Lon knew he would get to share the chicken so off he went, with a pail for the milk. About the time the porter got to the farmhouse, the train we were waiting for whizzed past and Lon was left. Our train began to move and everyone was worried how Lon would ever get to us. The ever-helpful cowboys came to the rescue, and when the horses were unloaded one of the boys mounted his horse and led a horse for Lon to ride back. Everyone cheered when the pair came riding down the tracks, one with a pail of milk and the other with two fat chickens. Needless to say that after the night show the porter and the cowboy had their share of the chicken. Missie had a small kitchenet in her car and could cook anything she liked, and often after the show we had our snack in the car.

Often in the morning or after the afternoon show a couple of kids that were with the show and myself, would get our horses out for a ride into the country. One fine day, I think it was Decoration Day, we were riding out at the edge of the town and came across a race track where there was a grandstand full of people, waiting for the running race to start. Naturally we went in and were asked to enter the race, which we did. About the time we were ready to start we glanced up into the grandstand and whom should we see but Vernon Seaver's father, the chief of the cowboys, whose son was with us, and my uncle. We were a little embarrassed but there was nothing to do but race, which we did and won something in the race. All of the way back to the camp after the race we were wondering what would happen to us. Not a thing said, for we all had a good time.

Jimmie was often able to settle trouble between the Indians, because he could speak their language and was also very diplomatic. One day there was trouble after the Indians had been paid. They were chattering. Jimmie went to see what he could do about it. An Indian called Red Shirt told him that the Chief had borrowed a dollar from him, and did not want to pay it back. Jimmie asked the Chief what was wrong, and he said Red Shirt had borrowed a dollar from him and now he did not want to pay it back. The Indians were always paid in silver because they thought they had more money than if they had been paid in paper money. Jimmie got a silver dollar from the Chief, then he got one from Red Shirt and he paid both debts, and in a minute the Indians all thought the thing was fair so went on their way.

We arrived in the show town down east early one hot Sunday morning, but were not to give the show until Monday. There was a swimming pool not far from the show grounds. Some of the Indians had been drinking and, the first thing, went up town and got into an argument with some town boys and the police put the red men in jail. The officer with the show went to the chief of police of the town and promised to take care of the offenders, but the chief was very unreasonable and would not let the officer with the show have the men. In less than an hour some band boys and a few of the cowboys were in the swimming pool. The cowboys were lucky enough to drag a young boy out of the water, who was so near drowned that he would have died before they could have gotten a doctor. A cowboy that was in the water gave the lad first aid and saved him. The boy was none other than the son of the chief of police of the town, and when the boy's father found out what had happened he came to the management of the show and offered all kinds of apologies and released the Indians. When the chief found out that the owners and management of the show were real people and more than willing to be fair, he made friends with them and could not do enough for the show while they were in his town. When the chief wanted to pay the cowboy who saved his son's life, he refused by saying he was always willing to do a good turn when he could.

One day Jimmie had sent some clothes to a tailor to have them pressed and after the night show the clothes had not been delivered and Jimmie sent Lon for them. When the porter returned we heard loud talk outside of our car Jimmie went to see what was wrong. He found Lon having an argument with a town negro and wanted to know what it was all about. Lon said that the fellow wanted him to call him mister somebody and told Jimmie, "Mr. Butler, Mister Butler, I will Mister no nigger."

We had rain for two weeks at one time and business had been bad, and somehow one of the Buffalo Bill flat cars had been hooked on to our train one night, and painted on the side of the car was Buffalo Bill's Wild West and Major Lillie's Far East. One day Lon came into our car after a day of bad business and said, "Mr. Butler, I knows what is wrong with business, the name of this show is too long, for by the time people read the name of this show,

'Buffalo Bill's Wild West, Major Lillie's Far East, Young Buffalo's Wild West, Vernon C. Seaver's Far East and Hippodrome,' it's night and they can't come to the show."

When one is on the road all of the time, unless you know someone in a town, or write a letter, often one does not bother to even think what town they might be in. More than once I have heard someone on the outside of the car say at night, about the time the train was ready to leave, "What town is this?"

We were in Quebec and I wanted to go in parade just to see the town, and the boss hostler thought he would have some fun with me, and he gave me what they called an outrider to ride. The horse was a tall good-looking one that had been ridden by the officer of the show, that meant he would ride along by the side of the parade, to keep law and order. One thing, the show people in a well run show are not supposed to notice or talk to town people, and it is the officer's job to try to keep people away from the parade along with the help of the town police. This day I started out all right, but thought my horse was rather stubborn and hard to manage. The people who were near me in parade were having a good time seeing how long I could keep in line. After a while the horse got the bit between his teeth and decided he wanted to see what Young Buffalo was doing at the head of the parade, so up to the front we went at a good speed. We rode along for two or three blocks, then he decided he wanted to look after the calliope at the far end of the parade, so with the bit between his teeth back to the end of the parade we went, running like a jack rabbit. How many times we rode the length of the parade I do not know, and by the time we got near the lot I was well tired out and a cowboy changed horses with me, for I would have had to go several miles more for the outrider thought it was his duty to round up everyone and see to it that they watered their horse, before they were fed.

The officers and their wives of the company and Missie and Jimmie and myself ate in a small dining tent. We thought we had real good manners, except for throwing bones and things we did not want to eat out under the wall of the tent for the dogs to eat, that were usually on hand at meal time. Sundays and when we had a chance we went to a good hotel to eat for a change. We were in a good hotel to eat one day. Mr. Seaver had been away for a few days. Jimmie and Seaver were busy talking, and when one of them finished a chicken bone he threw it over his shoulder on the floor. The waiter picked up the bone and asked if he had dropped it. He had forgotten he was not in the dining tent. Mr. Seaver turned to the waiter and said, "I know better. Now if it was Frank here, he has lived in a tent so long he really doesn't know how to live in a house."

We had a horse named Dock. His duty was to go on errands for the office. Most anyone who needed to go places on business drove Dock. There was a boy called the buggy boy whose duty it was to care for Dock and drive the trip for whoever used it. He usually drove Missie from the train to the lot unless it was near enough for us to walk. The money was usually counted and deposited after the afternoon show, and at night the treasurer drove to a bank to deposit the night show money, and if there were any suspicious persons around to see what might happen to the money, Missie went along with her little revolver, that she always carried in her purse.

One time we thought we would see if Dock could find his way to the train from the lot. It was a long way, and the horse had never been over the route before. Sure enough, he followed the torches and landed us safely at the train. Another time the buggy boy had not tied Dock and when he went to drive, the trap and horse were gone. We found that Dock had followed the torches and had gone to the train alone, and the train master had tied him to a car.

One of the first things that was done when the train arrived was for the route foreman to lay out the way to the lot by placing a lighted torch at each corner where they people were to turn. The torch was put at the right of the corner. The horses and other animals soon learned that the torch was meant for them and they knew what to do when they saw it.

We were in Cambridge, Maryland, with the show and somehow liked the people and the town, and all the rest of the season talked about building a home there sometime.

Young Buffalo was a figurehead with the show, and made a good Buffalo Bill. The show did a good business, but did not draw the crowds that the original show had.

The day the show closed Jimmie went to the head candy butcher and said, "Jack you started out in the spring with two dozen lemons floating in the lemonade and you only have ten now. What have you done with the rest?" A laugh for Jack. It was true they did use an acid to make lemonade and floated lemons and each day would throw away the slices of lemon that got soft.

After the close of the season the year I traveled all season, Missie and Jimmie went to Cambridge and bought a piece of ground along Choptank Bay and that winter began to build the dream house. They told their good friend Seaver that they could not go back with the show the next season. After I had been in school all winter I joined Missie and Jimmie in the summer of 1914 and we did enjoy the boating and fishing, and later in the fall, the hunting. The house was only a few hundred feet from the beautiful bay, and it was heavenly to sit on the porch and look over the bay and dream.

Jimmie had always wanted a strawberry bed, and had a nurseryman set a small bed. He thought that the plants should blossom right away and because they did not he thought the plants had not been set right, so every few days he would change some of them. He kept moving the young plants until he killed most of them.

Missie wanted a bird dog and they found someone who had Irish setter pups. Jimmie bought the last one to be sold and they named him Dave. The beautiful dog was a namesake of Dave Montgomery, of the team Montgomery and Stone. Jimmie had called one of his horses Fred for Fred Stone, and he thought Dave Montgomery should have an animal named for him. Dave had an interesting life and made many friends wherever he went.

Jimmie seemed to be very busy one afternoon and later he came in and handed me his *Hunter's Dream* he had just written.

Jimmie as he writes the Hunters Dream.

30
A HUNTER'S DREAM

A HUNTER NOW old and grey, sat musing on his sports of long ago; of the days when he was young, and of the dogs and guns he had owned, of his Juno, and Ponto, Diana, and his Bob; his Parker, Remington and Marlin, and sighed because his dogs were dead and hunting days were o'er and, while musing this, the call of Morpheus came and he went his way.

He slept and dreamed that he followed once again Diana to the rugged mountain rock ledge and timber thick, the home of the grouse. His dog is by his side; he follows the ledge mid the timber tall; the old dog glides away and quarters the mountain side, then crouching, trails and stands a statue, rigidly, the rock defying. Gracefully, and carefully climbing, deftly stepping he draws near, still, within range, the bird then flushed, he killed it with a shot. The dog has dropped and lies there closely crouching, waiting for the word to fetch. The word is given, off he bounds, and returning proudly places the dead bird beside his master on the ground. Thus in his dream he hunts again the partridge on the mountain side as he did in the days now passed and gone.

Then from the mountainside he passes over the hills to the familiar fields where the call of the quail is heard; on the lowland where feed the woodcock and snipe; thence to the pools and streams where rests the duck in her flight; on to the old familiar spring to quench from its sparkling flow his thirst, and resting there as in his boyhood days, looks again upon the mountain tall, every rock and tree, and running stream he knows, and they know him.

The tumbling waters to him again are singing, the trees beneath the gentle breezes blow, and the rocks their moss-gloved hands extend the friend of long ago. Then he from his well-filled pocket, takes the game and lovingly smoothes each grey feather down, places it beside him on the ground.

The old dog on the leaves lies watching and crawling close, licks his master's hand, but his looks plainly say, "Let us be off again." Soon he is on his way, following again the streams in its windings through meadow; watching the trout send forth its golden flash, as it darts from beneath the bank; listening to the chatter of the wren, as she starts from her resting place. And again there comes from the mountain that old familiar sound, the drum of the partridge as he beats his wings, his mate to find. Then turning he goes to hunt the quail; his dog is off and quickly circles the stubble field, to see if they are feeding there, then stops, sniffs the air, with his head well up, like a phantom gliding, carefully moving here and there, which indicates they are near. Then suddenly immovable, he stands pointing, proclaiming there they are! With gun firmly grasped with finger on the trigger, step by step, this hunter nearer draws. Then suddenly stops, the covey flushes, two shots, a bird for each in turn, and eagerly awaits the word; Hi On. Thus in fancy again he hunts the quail over the hills and stubble field of long ago.

Then on through thickets dark and damp, he in vision, wends his way to hunt the woodcock in her home of mud and clay. The dog before him carefully quartered in the mud, he sees the boring of that day. A point. The dog tells of a bird in front; then fluttering, whistling, whistling wings tell this hunter old and grey the woodcock through the elders flushing. Dropping on one knee he quickly sights a shot, the word his dog is off through mud and thicket, soon returning with the bird, long of bill and brown of back, a denizen of that elder patch.

By fancy, led to the burnt heather of the marsh for that bird of flight the English snipe, he presses on; the dog to the windward passing, better to sniff the air of the old marsh land. Soon he finds the game with head and tail outstretched, moves to where there rests a wisp of snipe, and there remains, to his side the hunter quickly steps, and with the old familiar "quack" they rise, turning on their wings, darting here and there in their flight, he waits as time has taught, until they straighten in their course, then pulls; a bird is down. The signal, a bound, and he is gathered in. So he in dreamland hunts this bird of flight till the coming of the night. As the evening shadows, of the mountain tell this hunter, that the clock of night is about to fall, he hears, in fancy once again, the old ducks calling at the pool where the waters tumble and fall. And thence he goes carefully crouching, with his dog behind him. Creeping to the bank where the pool is sheltered, best from view he is hiding, waits until he sees a pair of mallards in the distance coming. On they come with necks outstretched, then with wings set, they circle round, and in each circle close drawn until within range of shot. Right and left, a quacking and flopping of wings, a splash, and they are down. With a plunge his dog retrieves the ducks, placing them beside him on the bank, and thus in his dream he hunts the duck beside the pool and stream, until the call of the whippoorwill by him is heard, and from his vision light is passing, darkness coming. Then this hunter old shakes the grip of morpheus off, awakes and sighs because these days have passed, forever.

It was a hunter's dream of a day of hunting of long ago.

I THINK JIMMIE had been thinking of a day he had spent in England at Shrewsbury when he and Missie were so happy hunting and roaming over the lovely countryside. When Jimmie handed me *The Hunter's Dream* he seemed quite sad for he realized his best hunting days were over, and every word he had put into the dream has a deep meaning to him.

Those were happy days too we spent in Cambridge, except for the restless spirit Missie displayed and Jimmie and I were always wondering how long she would be satisfied to stay in the cozy place we had there, among such good friends. One thing we enjoyed so much was the open space we had to shoot in. We could shoot at mark out over the water, and in the open field there was a walnut tree with plenty of walnuts to shoot off the limbs.

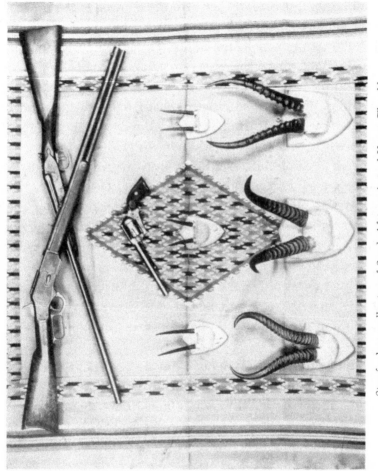

Six of a large collection of South African Animal Horns. The old gun Buffalo Bill gave the sister of Annie Oakley and another gun and pistol she used.

George Widows was the Englishman who had fallen in love with Missie while she was in England the first time, and had gone to South Africa and lost himself in the wilds when he had found out she was married. During all of the years Jimmie had written to him, and they had exchanged Christmas cards each year. George had spent most of his time hunting wild animals and collecting the horns.

During the summer of 1913 while we were in Cambridge, Maryland, Jimmie had a letter from Widows saying he was on his way to America to bring his collection of horns to Missie and Jimmie. I met him at the train when he came. He was a very interesting person and he had with him pictures, and many other things. The things that interested me were butterfly eggs and different kinds of seeds from wild plants. When he opened the box of horns there were twenty-five different kinds. There was a pair of rare Eland horns from the male that stands more than six feet high. The smallest horns were the Blowbok, from an adult male only twelve inches high. When Widows got to the U. S. custom officer as he entered the states and told him that the horns were not for sale, that they were a gift for Annie Oakley and her husband, the officer did not charge him duty. The Englishman was a real gentleman and wanted to see something of America, and when fall came he went to Florida and died shortly after. That same summer Missie went to New York and gave a good exhibition in the society circus that was given for charity and she thoroughly enjoyed it.

In the wintertime Missie and Jimmie were ready for hunting in North Carolina and they lived at the Carolina Hotel in Pinehurst, where they enjoyed the gun club, and she gave some interesting exhibitions, and got some ladies to shoot at the club who had never tried to shoot before.

During World War I when the Red Cross was collecting money, Missie and Jimmie did some shooting in the camps in U. S. and Dave the setter worked with them. Jimmie would have him sit up and put an apple on his head and Missie shot it into bits and Dave caught the largest pieces in his mouth and ran away to eat them. When they shot at gun clubs Jimmie would ask for a check or a bill, and promise to match it if he hid it and Dave could not find it. He let Dave smell the money and Missie would blindfold Dave, Jimmie hid the money any place the donor suggested. Dave always found the secret place, and in that way they collected money for the Red Cross.

Keeping house was not an easy task for Missie. She was too particular and could not get help to please her. She sold the house in Cambridge and gave most of her things away, and they went back into hotels to live. The late fall of 1921 Missie and Jimmie decided to go to Leesburg, Florida, for the winter. They had gone to Philadelphia to shop and Jimmie met a friend who was going to Leesburg and he suggested that they meet him in Jacksonville and ride down to Leesburg with them. The friend's chauffeur met the two couples as planned, and on the way they went onto a soft shoulder on a new road and landed in the ditch. The result was Missie was hurt badly. Her hip out of joint and her ankle broken, she spent months in one hospital or another and never could walk without a brace on her foot. Jimmie was hurt internally. After the accident they got to Leesburg, and one day while Jimmie had Dave out for a walk a friend drove his car around a corner just as Dave started to chase a squirrel and Dave was killed instantly. They buried the dog by the side of Bob the dog that had been bitten by a rattlesnake several years before, while they were hunting in Leesburg.

It was very hard for Missie to be an invalid after having been so active all of her life, and always wanting to do something for the other fellow, and to the day she died she was thinking of someone else. No matter what fame or fortune came to her she never forgot her family and old friends.

After the accident she felt she would not live long, and she thought no one would want the gold medals she had won all over the world shooting, so she melted them up and sold the gold for something over a hundred dollars and gave the money to a children's hospital in the south.

Missie told me over and over again interesting stories of her life. She wanted me to sometime write a story of her life. She wanted to go back near where she was born to die, and she spoke of death as the path leading to the open gates of God's Great World. I had heard her pray often when she was tired and not so well, "Oh that I might live over again those days of simplicity, when God was consulted, and asked to guide the little family through each day, and keep them through the silent watches of the night. It far surpassed being bowed to and complimented by crowned heads of all the world, though I appreciated in after years the homage paid me by them."

Missie's wants were simple and she wished to be alone when the end came, so she went back to the little town of Greenville, Ohio, where she could have her good Dr. Husted. She called my mother to her and got all settled in a comfortable room with a nurse to look after her and then told Mother she was ready to go when her time came and she waited not long. Rev. Wessel told me of the many times he called to see her and how she told him she had longed for the simple life again. She wanted Jimmie to go south for the winter because she thought he would be better there. He left her with a heavy heart and only went because he thought he was pleasing her. He went to Newark, New Jersey, on his way South. While Jimmie was in Newark he went with a friend to the Smith Gun Club to shoot and took his trunk full of guns. When he came back to his hotel instead of the trunk going there it went to the friend's office and as far as I know it is still there, and the story of the guns will never be told. My mother had helped him pack the guns and she knew how many were in the trunk. Jimmie was ill and wired me to meet him and go on to Pinehurst with him. I had him come to Detroit until I could arrange to go with him. He was never able to leave for the South, and in less than two months Missie died, and he was too ill to go to her, so I stayed with him to comfort him as best I could. When I told him that Missie was gone he told me that she wanted to be cremated but that he did not want to be. Missie had made her own funeral arrangements, and she had the silver loving cup (that had been given to her by the people of France) fixed with a screw top and her ashes were placed in it and kept and buried eighteen days later with Jimmie. He never ate a bite after she went. He said he could not swallow. His death was

After the wreck and her hair had turned white in seventeen hours.

a result of the accident they had been in on the way to Leesburg, and his heart was broken when she was gone.

When Jimmie came to me and went into the room I had fixed for him, he said, "You may fix a room up as you like, but after all it's the people in it that count." Many times he had said, he knew he could depend upon me, for if ever Missie died before he did he knew he would be helpless.

A week before Missie died she sent for me, and I went to her and had three days with her, and her main thought was for me to look after Jimmie and the promise I made I did not need to keep long.

They had both made the request that instead of sending flowers to the funeral, they would like the friends to remember some charity and I have often wondered how many did. They were buried from the home of dear friends, Mr. and Mrs. Fred Grote, in Greenville. After years of busy lives, the little private funeral was a simple one, as they had wished it to be. They were buried in the little country cemetery near Brock, Ohio, Thanksgiving day 1926. As we turned from the graves a relative of mine, W. E. Drill (whom my uncle had hunted with in his younger days) said, "Twenty years ago today Jimmie and I went by this very spot from a day's hunting." So we left Missie and Jimmie in the happy hunting land.

The last thing that Jimmie wrote was:

WHAT DID YOU DO

Did you give him a lift? He's a brother of Man,
And bearing about all the burden he can.
Did you give him a smile, he's downcast and blue
And a smile might have helped him battle it through;
Did you give him your hand? He was slipping down hill
And the world, so I fancied was using him ill;
Did you give him a word, did you show him the road
Or did you just let him go on with his load?

Did you help him along? He's a sinner like you,
But the grasp of your hand might have carried him through

Did you bid him good cheer? Just a word and a smile
Were what he most needed that last weary mile.
Do you know what he bore in that burden of cares
That is every man's load and that sympathy shares?
Did you try to find out what he needed from you,
Or did you leave him to battle it through?

Do you know what it meant to be losing the fight
When a lift in time might have set everything right?
Do you know what it meant, just the clasp of the hand
When a man has born about all a man ought to stand?
Did you ask what it was; why the quivering lip?
Were you brother of his when the time came to be?
Did you offer to help him or didn't you see?

Don't you know it's a part of a brother of man
To find what the grief is and help what you can?
Did you stop when he asked you to give him a lift?
Or were you so busy you left him to shift?
Oh I know what you mean, what you say may be true,
But the test of your manhood is what did you do?
Did you reach out a hand did you show him the road?
Or did you just let him go on with his load.

FRANK E. BUTLER

Just before the accident that caused the death of Missie and Jimmie five years later.

COACHWHIP PUBLICATIONS

COACHWHIPBOOKS.COM

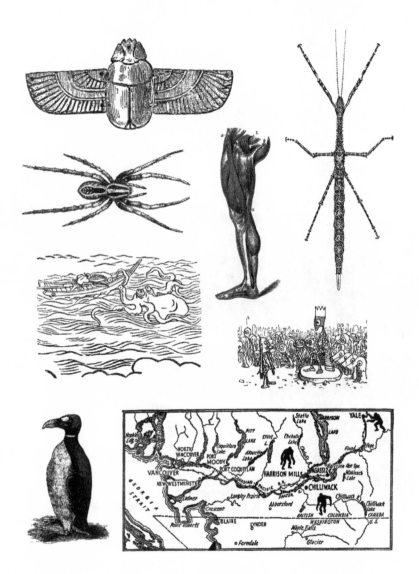

COACHWHIP PUBLICATIONS
ALSO AVAILABLE

How to Draw Horses
ISBN 978-1-61646-190-4

COACHWHIP PUBLICATIONS

COACHWHIPBOOKS.COM

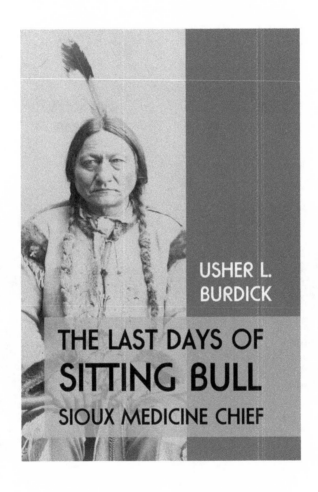

The Last Days of Sitting Bull
ISBN 978-1-61646-100-3

PRIMITIVE
AND PIONEER
SPORTS
FOR RECREATION TODAY

Bernard S. Mason

Primitive and Pioneer Sports
ISBN 978-1-61646-126-3

Printed in the USA
CPSIA information can be obtained
at www.ICGtesting.com
LVHW040001190923
758289LV00007B/769